101
QUESTIONS
ABOUT BLOOD AND CIRCULATION
... WITH ANSWERS STRAIGHT
FROM THE HEART

101

QUESTIONS ABOUT

BLOOD AND CIRCULATION

. . . WITH ANSWERS STRAIGHT FROM THE HEART

· · · ·

FAITH HICKMAN BRYNIE

· · · ·

Twenty-First Century Books

BROOKFIELD, CONNECTICUT

Published by Twenty-First Century Books
A Division of The Millbrook Press, Inc.
2 Old New Milford Road
Brookfield, CT 06804
www.millbrookpress.com

Library of Congress Cataloging-in-Publication Data
Brynie, Faith Hickman, 1946-
101 questions about blood and circulation ... with answers straight from
the heart / Faith Hickman Brynie.
    p. cm.
Includes bibliographical references and index.
ISBN 0-7613-1455-5 (lib. bdg.)
1. Cardiovascular system—Juvenile literature. 2. Blood—Circulation—
Juvenile literature. [1. Circulatory system—Miscellanea. 2. Blood—
Miscellanea. 3. Heart—Miscellanea. 4. Questions and answers.] I. One
hundred and one questions about blood and circulation ... with answers
straight from the heart.
QP103 .B79 2001
612.1—dc21   00-032570

"Hormones" by Pauline Williamson reprinted by permission of the author.

Cover illustration by Anne Canevari Green

Photographs courtesy of Peter Arnold, Inc.: pp. 10 (© Ed Reschke), 60
(© David Scharf), 99 (© SIU); Phototake, Inc.: p. 21 (© Dr. Dennis
Kunkel); De Grummond Children's Literature Collection, The University
of Southern Mississippi: p. 36; Photo Researchers, Inc.: pp. 44 (left, ©
1993 SIU; right, SPL), 62 (© Ken Eward), 105 (SPL); Penn State
Geisinger Health System: p. 57 (top); Baylor College of Medicine: p. 57
(bottom); Visuals Unlimited: pp. 66 (© SIU), 82 (© C. P. Hickman); 85
(© Veronika Burmeister), 102 (© Fred E. Hossler); Glaxowell: p. 101; ©
Sabina Dowell: p. 144

CONTENTS

ACKNOWLEDGMENTS

Wrote Robert Lynd in 1959: "The great pleasure of ignorance is the pleasure of asking questions. The man who has lost this pleasure or exchanged it for the pleasure of dogma, which is the pleasure of answering, is already beginning to stiffen." This author—mindful of Lynd's cautions and happily learning more daily from the questions than from the answers—wishes to thank those who have so kindly provided both.

The author is grateful to the following teachers and their students for the questions they contributed to this volume: Mary Jane Davis, Red Bank Catholic High School, Red Bank, NJ; Tim Culp, Arroyo Grande High School, Arroyo Grande, CA; Jill Losee-Hoehlein, Great Bridge High School, Chesapeake, VA; and Mark Stephansky, Whitman-Hanson Regional High School, Whitman, MA. Thanks also to Kathy Frame of the National Association of Biology Teachers for making their involvement possible.

Sincere appreciation goes to Dr. Louis Bloomfield, Professor of Physics, University of Virginia, Charlottesville, and the author of *How Things Work: The Physics of Everyday Life*, for his assistance with water pumps.

The author greatly appreciates the thorough and thoughtful critical reviews prepared by Dr. Jack Davis, internist and cardiologist in private practice, Kalispell, Montana; and Dr. Upinderjit Sidhu, a physician in Weston, Connecticut.

Thanks also to perfusionists Debra Douglass and Bob Dyga for their in-depth interviews and to Pat Kaiser and Jennifer Fuller for arranging their involvement.

Special thanks, as always, to Amy Shields, for being the most supportive and positive editor a writer could hope for. And finally the deepest appreciation to those the author counts on most: Ann for her spirit, Tammy for her nurturing, and Lloyd for his patience, understanding, and unfailing good humor.

Keep those questions coming.

FOREWORD

Life is a continuous struggle against entropy. You know entropy. It's the natural state of things: the tendency of all systems to become increasingly disorganized over time unless energy is injected into them. Bedrooms do it. Left to their own devices, they get messier and messier until you clean them. Tanks of fuel that power a car do it. They run dry and must be refilled. Their energy is lost into the universe as the random molecular motion we call heat. Bodies do it. Without a fresh supply of food, water, and oxygen, they perish. In biological terms, life is the temporary reversal of disorder.

If you were a single-celled amoeba oozing your way around a pond, your battle against entropy would be relatively simple. You would get your food and oxygen directly from the water, through your cell membrane. You could dump your waste materials into the water the same way.

If, however, you happen to be more complex than an amoeba, your battle against entropy is more complex too. Being made of more than

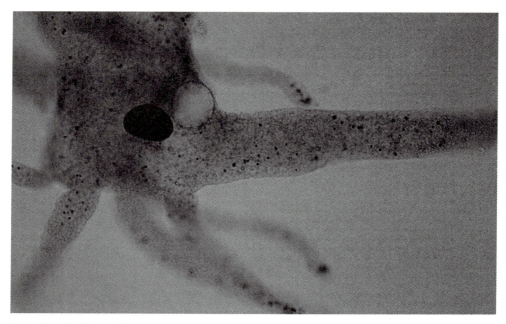

A single-celled amoeba

one cell complicates things. Your cells cannot gain food and oxygen directly from the environment because most lie buried deep inside other cell layers. Far from any source of food, water, and oxygen—and equally far from a convenient garbage dump—internal cells need a supply, delivery, and waste removal strategy.

An engineer injects materials and energy into a mechanical system with pumps, pipes, and valves. Evolution has done the same for many-celled organisms. As blood circulates in the human body—pushed along by that powerful pump the heart—it picks up food and water from the small intestine and oxygen from the lungs. It gets rid of carbon dioxide through the lungs and waste products such as urea through the kidneys. The bloodstream is also a corridor for chemical communication between the brain and other parts of the body. Hormones carry messages back and forth. They "command the troops" in the war against entropy, whether speeding the heart rate when danger looms or storing energy for future skirmishes.

In this book, you'll learn about blood and how your circulatory system works. You'll get answers "straight from the heart" to some important questions you may have wondered about. Perhaps you will answer a few you never thought of before. Either way, you'll gain knowledge—the best weapon of all in your successful battle against entropy.

CHAPTER ONE

14
QUESTIONS
THAT SHOULD
COME FIRST

The human heart has hidden treasure,
In secret kept, in silence sealed.

• CHARLOTTE BRONTË •

What Does My Circulatory System Do? If your circulatory system had a motto, it would be the same as the police department's: "To serve and protect." Circulating blood serves by delivering supplies—nutrients, water, and oxygen— to every body cell. It also carries away poisonous wastes. Blood carries toxic carbon dioxide gas to the lungs, from which it is exhaled into the air. It carries nitrogen-containing wastes to the liver. There they are converted to urea, which the bloodstream carries to the kidneys. The kidneys make urine from urea, ammonia, and other harmful substances dissolved in excess water.

Circulating blood *protects* the body in several ways. It carries hormones from where they are made to their sites of action. Hormones regulate body functions. For example, insulin produced in the pancreas maintains safe levels of sugar in the blood, while thyroxine manufactured in the thyroid gland controls the rate of energy release in cells.

Another *protective* activity is fighting infections. White blood cells recognize, attack, and destroy foreign invaders such as disease-causing viruses and bacteria. Some dangers—such as cancer cells that begin dividing out of control—arise within the body itself. When they do, certain cells and molecules in the blood stand ready to annihilate them before they can multiply or spread.

Human life depends on circulating blood in the right amounts and of the right chemical makeup. So important are the blood's functions that it contains its own loss prevention mechanism. Sustain an injury and your blood will clot. Bleeding will stop. That's another way your blood *protects* you.

What Are the Parts of My Circulatory System?

We usually think of the circulatory system as the heart that pumps blood and the vessels that carry it.

Four separate chambers form the human heart. The two at the top, the atria (singular is atrium), receive blood through veins. The lower chambers, called ventricles, pump blood away from the heart through arteries. Four valves within the heart maintain a one-way flow of blood through the chambers and into the arteries. Valves in the veins keep blood flowing back toward the heart.

While the "pump-and-pipes" view of the circulatory system is accurate, it's also limited. In truth, circulation links all the systems of the body, and many other organs help maintain the blood's chemistry.

For example:

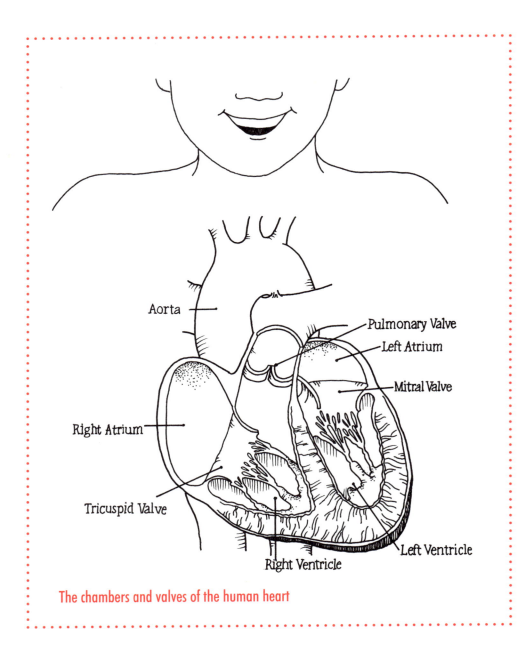

Aorta

Pulmonary Valve

Left Atrium

Mitral Valve

Right Atrium

Tricuspid Valve

Left Ventricle

Right Ventricle

The chambers and valves of the human heart

Bone marrow. If you think of bones as hard, dry, and dead, think again. Living bone is a hubbub of activity, from its outer layers jammed with nerves and blood vessels to its spongy interior, the marrow. Nerves and capillaries run through the corridors of the inner bone and into the gelatin-like material at the center. Here all types of blood cells are made, including the red cells that carry oxygen, the white cells that fight infections, and the platelets that are essential to clotting.

Liver. If a body organ could get an Academy Award for "most versatile actor," the liver would win hands down. It performs some 500 different functions, all of them vital to health.[1] One important job is the filtering of toxins and bacteria from the blood. That filtering occurs at the incredible rate of 2.5 pints (about 1.2 liters) every minute.[2]

The liver also collects and stores vitamins A, B, D, E, and K. It removes them from the bloodstream when the supply is ample and releases them later, when supplies run low. It makes vitamin B_{12} available for the manufacture of red blood cells. The iron it stores goes into making hemoglobin, the oxygen-carrying molecule in red blood cells.

Your liver provides all body cells with food energy when they need it. When your blood-sugar level is high—just after a meal, for example—the liver changes excess glucose sugar into glycogen, which it stores for later. When blood-sugar levels dip, the liver quickly changes glycogen back to glucose and releases it into the blood. The storage of glycogen is the main reason you don't need to eat constantly to keep going all day.

Your liver also maintains the reserve of blood that serves the body whenever rest ends and strenuous activity begins. When you lie down or sit quietly, about a quarter of your blood stays in your liver.[3] But jump up to run outside, and blood from the liver immediately rushes the blood into circulation.

Both the liver and the spleen break down and recycle dead red blood cells. The liver converts hemoglobin into bilirubin, a waste product that is normally excreted in the urine. Disease or malfunction of the liver can cause bilirubin to accumulate in the body. It turns the skin yellow, a condition called jaundice.

Endocrine glands. Along with the nervous system, the endocrine glands are the body's main regulators of function. Also called ductless glands, the endocrines in the head, neck, and abdomen manufacture hormones and release them directly into the bloodstream. Hormones travel through the blood to other parts of the body, where they cause some body process or chemical reaction to speed up or slow down.

For example, the adrenal glands, which sit atop the kidneys, produce hormones that regulate the use of proteins, fats, and glucose as food and raw materials in cells. They also make epinephrine (adrenaline). This powerful hormone accelerates breathing and heart rate. It also speeds the release of energy in times of emergency, danger, or stress. (For more detail on hormones, see Table 1 on page 150.)

Lungs. Every day, about 5,000 gallons (nearly 20,000 liters) of air move in and out of your lungs.[4] The contraction of the chest muscles surrounding the ribs and the rise and fall of the diaphragm (a sheet of muscle that lies beneath the lungs) cause inhaling and exhaling.

The nitrogen and rare gases move in and back out again, unchanged. Not so with carbon dioxide and oxygen. Their concentrations change. Some of the oxygen from the air enters your bloodstream, while carbon dioxide is expelled in the air you exhale. As a result, you exhale less oxygen and more carbon dioxide than you inhaled. The exchange occurs across the thin walls of capillaries (the smallest blood vessels) in the alveoli (tiny air sacs of the lungs).

Kidneys. These two bean-shaped organs lie in your abdomen near the small of your back. Although smaller than your fist, they filter a bit more than a quart (about a liter) of blood every 10 minutes. That's 150 quarts (140 liters) a day![5] The kidneys remove toxic wastes from the blood, but that's not all they do. They also keep the blood's fluid content steady by excreting or conserving water. The kidneys regulate lev-

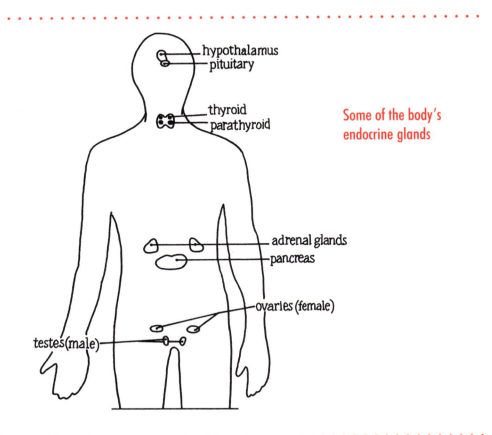

hypothalamus
pituitary

thyroid
parathyroid

Some of the body's
endocrine glands

adrenal glands
pancreas

ovaries (female)

testes (male)

els of sodium and potassium in the blood. They recycle minerals and nutrients.

Small intestine. Digestion in the stomach and small intestine breaks food down into its chemical constituents:

- glucose from carbohydrate foods, such as bread or potatoes;

- amino acids from protein foods, such as meat or milk;

- and diglycerides, free fatty acids, and glycerol from fatty foods, such as butter, margarine, or oils.

Tiny fingerlike projections called villi line the walls of the small intestine. They greatly increase its inner surface area. Molecules from digested foods pass across the membranes of the villi into the capillaries that lie within. Water from food passes into the blood from both the small and the large intestine.

Perhaps this discussion has convinced you that studying the circulatory system in isolation from all the others is only a matter of convenience. All body systems depend on blood and on the heart action that propels it. The blood, in turn, relies on the body's other systems to maintain its composition.

What's My Circulatory System Made Of?

Like the rest of you, your heart and blood vessels are mostly protein. Protein molecules are chains of smaller molecules called amino acids. Twenty different kinds of amino acids make up human proteins. Atoms of carbon, hydrogen, oxygen, nitrogen, and sometimes phosphorus and sulfur combine to form amino acids. There's nothing special about these atoms, but the arrangement of amino acids in proteins is special. Every kind of protein is different because of the number, order, and arrangement of amino acids within it. The amino-acid sequence determines the shape a protein molecule will twist and fold into. The shape, in turn, determines the job a protein will do.

Your heart is a muscle. It is made of proteins that contract (shorten and thicken), just as the muscles in your arms and legs do. The walls of arteries contain a lot of muscle protein, too. That makes them flexible (when normal and healthy), so that they expand rhythmically with each

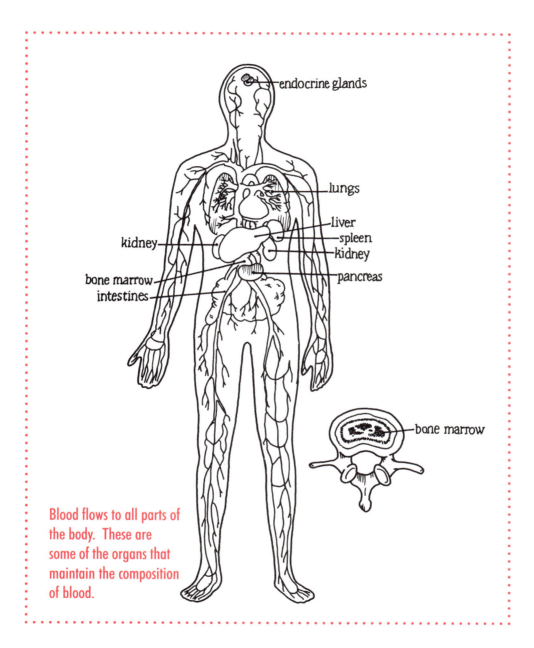

endocrine glands

lungs

liver

spleen

kidney

kidney

pancreas

bone marrow

intestines

bone marrow

Blood flows to all parts of the body. These are some of the organs that maintain the composition of blood.

beat of the heart and the passage of blood through them. Veins are less muscular, and do not pulse with the heartbeat.

What Is Blood?
That red stuff in your veins and arteries is a complex "soup." More than half its volume is plasma, a straw-colored solution that's over 90 percent water. Dissolved in it are many different kinds of molecules, including proteins, enzymes, hormones, and glucose (the sugar that supplies energy to cells). Salts dissolved in plasma—such as sodium, potassium, and calcium—occur in minute concentrations, but they are essential to the work of muscles and nerves and to the construction and maintenance of bones and teeth.

Proteins in plasma do many jobs. They carry away wastes and maintain water concentrations in both blood and cells. They keep the blood's acid-base balance. They regulate metabolism, the rate of energy used in cells. Also, plasma acts much like circulating coolant in an automobile radiator. During periods of heavy exercise, the muscles produce an extra load of heat. The heat is transferred to blood, carried in plasma, and expelled through the skin and lungs.

Three particularly important plasma proteins are albumin, globulin, and fibrinogen. Albumin (also found in egg whites) helps maintain blood volume and pressure. Globulin is important in fighting disease. Fibrinogen is essential to clotting. When fibrinogen and the many other clotting factors are removed from plasma, the product is called serum.

Cells make up the rest of blood's volume. Erythrocytes—red blood cells—look like donuts that didn't quite manage a hole. Elastic and flexible, red cells can squeeze through the narrowest capillaries. There, hemoglobin releases the oxygen that sustains every body cell. You have

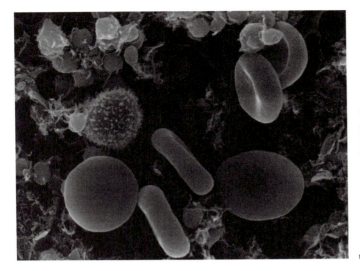

An electron micrograph of the living cells within blood, magnified 9900x.

about 25 billion red blood cells circulating at any one time.[6] With some 280 million molecules of hemoglobin packed inside them[7] —each capable of carrying four oxygen molecules—the oxygen-carrying capacity of red cells is enormous.

White blood cells, or leukocytes, make up about 10 percent of the total volume of blood.[8] They combat diseases and fight infections. Unlike red cells, white cells can move on their own. They ooze through capillary walls. In surrounding tissues, they locate and engulf invading viruses and bacteria. (For more on the many types of leukocytes, see Table 2, page 152.)

Each cubic millimeter of blood contains between 200,000 and 400,000 platelets.[9] These tiny cells collect at the site of a wound and stick together, creating a plug that stops further bleeding. They also react with clotting factors to convert fibrinogen into a mesh of fibrin threads. The threads trap other cells and seal the wound completely.

Your heart is a pump. Like a pump that lifts water from a well, the heart uses differences in pressure to fill a chamber, then force fluid from it. The heart also uses valves that open and close to keep blood moving in one direction.

Your heart is a flexible chamber. Blood flows in when the heart muscle is relaxed, and a valve closes behind it. Contraction of the cham-

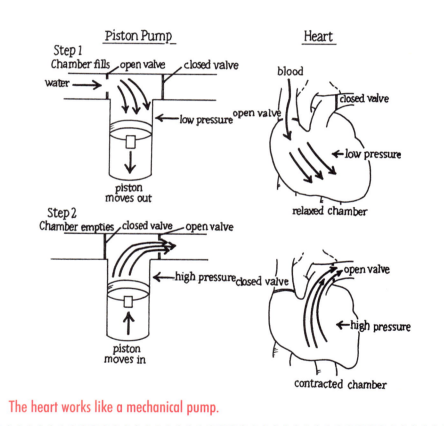

The heart works like a mechanical pump.

ber forces blood out through a vessel. Again a valve closes, preventing the blood from flowing backward into the now-relaxed chamber.

The heart is actually two pumps, since the circulation of blood to the body from the heart's left side is separate from the circulation of blood to the lungs on the heart's right side. But, one pump or two, the action is the same. Compression of the ventricles increases pressure. Valves keep blood moving always forward, never backward.

Every pump needs a driving force, and your heart is no exception. Mechanical pumps rely on engines driven by electricity or some other fuel. Your heart derives its power from food. It takes the equivalent of five watts of electricity to power your heart. For comparison, an ordinary flashlight bulb uses 0.75 watts. The heart's electrical power could illuminate about seven flashlights. That may not sound like much, but your heart uses enough energy in one hour to raise a medium-size car three feet (nearly a meter) off the ground.[10]

What Path Does Blood Follow as It Moves Through My Body?

Imagine yourself as a single red blood cell traveling from the heart to a big toe and back again. Since your journey is a circuit, your trip might be said to begin anywhere, but you are "at your best" in the heart's left atrium. Why? Because that's where you carry a fresh supply of oxygen, just collected from the lungs. (More about that later.)

From the left atrium, you tumble into the left ventricle. You cannot return to the left atrium because the mitral valve closes behind you. The left ventricle contracts powerfully and launches you into the aorta. That's the main artery that supplies blood to the torso, arms, and legs. It also branches into the carotid artery, which moves blood upward into the

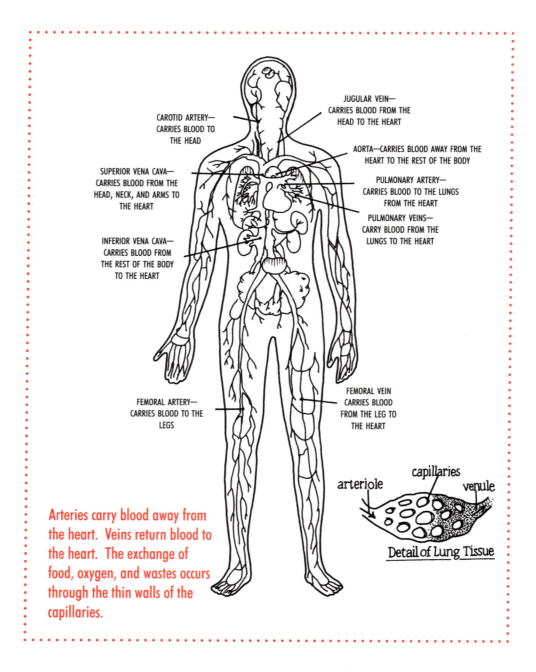

CAROTID ARTERY—
CARRIES BLOOD TO
THE HEAD

JUGULAR VEIN—
CARRIES BLOOD FROM THE
HEAD TO THE HEART

AORTA—CARRIES BLOOD AWAY FROM THE
HEART TO THE REST OF THE BODY

SUPERIOR VENA CAVA—
CARRIES BLOOD FROM THE
HEAD, NECK, AND ARMS TO
THE HEART

PULMONARY ARTERY—
CARRIES BLOOD TO THE LUNGS
FROM THE HEART

PULMONARY VEINS—
CARRY BLOOD FROM THE
LUNGS TO THE HEART

INFERIOR VENA CAVA—
CARRIES BLOOD FROM
THE REST OF THE BODY
TO THE HEART

FEMORAL ARTERY—
CARRIES BLOOD TO THE
LEGS

FEMORAL VEIN
CARRIES BLOOD
FROM THE LEG TO
THE HEART

arteriole

capillaries

venule

Detail of Lung Tissue

Arteries carry blood away from the heart. Veins return blood to the heart. The exchange of food, oxygen, and wastes occurs through the thin walls of the capillaries.

head and the cardiac arteries, which supply the heart muscle itself. Once in the aorta, you cannot flow back into the left ventricle, because the aortic valve has snapped shut behind you.

In the aorta, the push of the heart is still strong, and you move swiftly into smaller and smaller arteries. As you move farther away from the heart, the speed of your travel slows. The arteries continue narrowing, eventually branching into the smallest arteries, called arterioles. Finally, the blood vessels are so tiny that you and the other red blood cells must squeeze through in single file. These are the capillaries.

In one such tiny capillary, you have work to do. You give up the oxygen molecule you have been carrying since your trip from the lungs. The oxygen moves out through the capillary walls and enters the cells of your big toe. There, the oxygen is used to release energy from food. That energy keeps the cells of your big toe alive. After your cargo of oxygen is released, you are ready for your return load. You accept a molecule of carbon dioxide, a waste product created from the energy-releasing activities of those same toe cells.

All around you, other exchanges are taking place. Molecules of glucose and amino acids are "leaking" out of the capillaries and into the toe cells. Those toe cells will use glucose as an energy source. Amino acids, the building blocks of protein, will provide the raw materials for cellular maintenance and repair.

Traffic flows in both directions. Molecules of waste, including urea and ammonia, move through the capillary walls and into the fluid that surrounds you. The bloodstream will carry these wastes to the kidneys, just as you will carry carbon dioxide to the lungs.

You're not the only kind of blood cell active in the capillaries. As you look around, you see many different kinds of leukocytes (white blood cells) moving out through the capillary walls. They will patrol the toe cells for disease-causing invaders and gobble up any that they find. You also see antibodies, the Y-shaped proteins that can latch onto microbes and mark them for destruction by enzymes. If the toe has been cut or scraped, platelets and blood proteins will move to the site, starting the complex process of clotting the blood and healing the wound.

From the capillaries, your return journey to the heart begins. You move—much more slowly now—into vessels that become increasingly wider: first, the tiniest veins, called venules, then the much larger veins. In the veins, the pulse of the heart's pumping action is gone. Muscle action moves you through the veins of a leg. Every centimeter (about one-half inch), a valve closes behind you,[11] keeping you moving ever upward (assuming the body you serve is standing and not hanging from the ceiling). Eventually, you tumble into the inferior vena cava, a major vein that returns blood from the lower part of the body to the heart. That vein soon joins the superior vena cava from the head and empties into the vena cava itself, the vein that returns all blood to the heart.

You return not to the heart's left atrium, but to its right. Since you now carry waste carbon dioxide, you must travel to the lungs for a fresh supply of oxygen before you are ready to serve the body again. From the right atrium, you enter the right ventricle. The tricuspid valve closes behind you, preventing you from returning to the atrium. The contraction of the heart's right ventricle propels you into the pulmonary artery, and the pulmonary valve immediately snaps shut behind you.

All around you now move red cells laden with waste carbon dioxide. The pulmonary artery branches into smaller arterioles and eventually into tiny capillaries that run through the alveoli of the lungs. So thin are the capillaries and the walls of these air sacs that gas molecules move freely through the membranes. In a flash, your load of carbon dioxide seeps out into the alveoli, and a fresh load of oxygen moves in. Now you begin another trip to the heart, traveling first through small venules and then through the large pulmonary vein that empties into the heart's left atrium.

Your round trip is complete. You've traveled at speeds up to ten miles an hour.[12] In about 20 seconds,[13] you delivered oxygen, returned carbon dioxide, and picked up fresh oxygen. You are ready for another circuit of the body.

How Are Arteries and Veins Different?

Arteries carry blood away from the heart. Healthy arteries and arterioles are both strong and supple. They are made of layers of muscle, elastic, and fibrous tissues, interlined with a slippery cell layer that keeps blood flowing freely and prevents arteries from leaking. Normal arteries expand when the heart contracts. Their movement supplements the pumping action of the heart and helps keep blood moving.

Veins return blood to the heart. Also made of three layers, they are thinner than arteries and less muscular. They are also less flexible.

Major differences include:

ARTERIES	VEINS
Invisible through skin, usually lying within muscle and close to the bone.	Visible in many places, including the inner arm, hands, feet, legs, chest, and anywhere they lie close to the skin's surface.
Carry oxygenated blood (except the pulmonary artery to the lungs).	Carry deoxygenated blood (except the pulmonary vein from the lungs to the heart).
Keep their shape when blood pressure drops.	Collapse when blood pressure drops.
No valves.	Valves.
Pulse with the heartbeat.	Do not pulse with the heartbeat.
Generally named for the organ supplied with oxygen. For example, the renal artery supplies the kidneys, and the cardiac arteries, the heart muscle itself.	Sometimes named for the organ from which they remove carbon dioxide. For example, the renal vein; but the jugular vein drains blood from the head.
When injured, bleed rapidly with a pulse.	When injured, bleed slowly without a pulse.

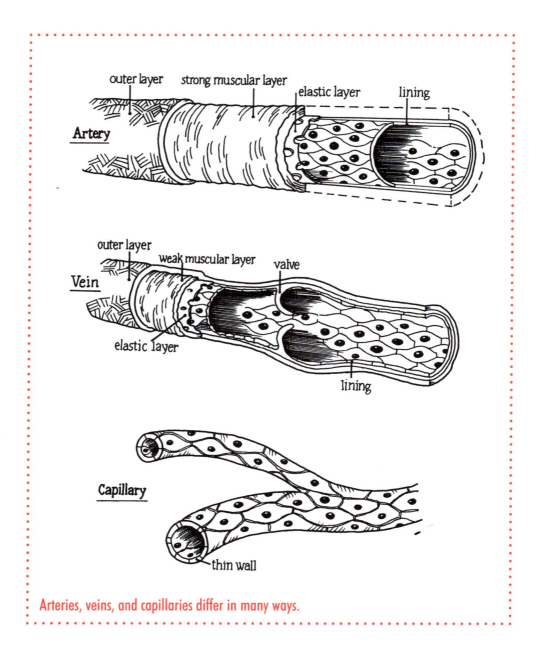

Artery — outer layer, strong muscular layer, elastic layer, lining

Vein — outer layer, weak muscular layer, valve, elastic layer, lining

Capillary — thin wall

Arteries, veins, and capillaries differ in many ways.

How Big Are My Heart and Blood Vessels?

A healthy adult heart is about the size of a fist and weighs about 11 ounces (a little over 300 grams). The heart of a trained athlete may weigh about a pound or 450 grams.[14]

The aorta is the largest artery. It measures about an inch (2.5 centimeters) in diameter. The smallest arterioles are only 0.02 inches (half a millimeter) across.[15] Capillaries average about one-thousandth of a millimeter.[16] That's less than one-tenth of the width of a human hair.[17]

How Does My Blood Exchange Materials with My Cells?

About 99 percent of the length of the circulatory system is capillaries,[18] and that's where the real work is done. The walls of the capillaries are only one cell thick. Molecules move freely through such thin walls. How does the process work? Think about what happens when you drop a little food coloring into a glass of water. Gradually, the color spreads out. The molecules of color move from where they are greatest in number (their area of greatest concentration) to where they are fewest (least concentration).

The same thing happens across the walls of capillaries. In working cells, the concentrations of oxygen and glucose fall. Concentrations of carbon dioxide and nitrogen-containing wastes rise. When fresh blood arrives in the capillaries, glucose and oxygen move from the blood where their concentration is high into the cells where their concentration is low. For the same reason, carbon dioxide and other wastes move from body cells into the blood.

Skin, kidneys, and lungs remove waste materials from the blood.

Your skin contains some three to five million sweat glands.[19] These glands empty directly onto the skin's outer surface through pores. Sweat (perspiration) is about 99 percent water.[20] It carries in it small amounts of sodium, potassium, and magnesium. Sweat helps get rid of excess heat. It also rids the body of some waste materials, including the poison urea, which is eliminated in greater quantities through the kidneys.

The functional unit of your kidneys is a microscopic ball of capillaries surrounded by a capsule. Each kidney contains about a million of

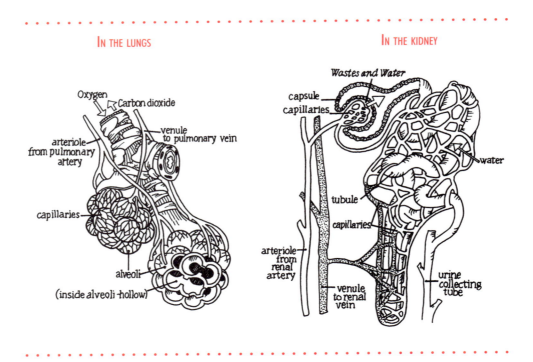

IN THE LUNGS

Oxygen
Carbon dioxide
arteriole from pulmonary artery
venule to pulmonary vein
capillaries
alveoli
(inside alveoli—hollow)

IN THE KIDNEY

Wastes and Water
capsule
capillaries
water
tubule
capillaries
arteriole from renal artery
venule to renal vein
urine collecting tube

these ball and capsule units.[21] Certain proteins, excess salts and vitamins, waste materials, and water molecules move out of capillaries and into the capsule. Normally, the proteins and a lot of the water diffuse back into the bloodstream, leaving wastes and water behind to form urine.

In the lungs, the waste is neither solid nor liquid, but a gas, carbon dioxide. The alveoli—about 600 million of them in each lung[22] —are surrounded by a dense network of capillaries. The walls of the capillaries and alveoli are so thin that carbon dioxide molecules pass through them.

Where and How Does My Body Make Blood?

Within the bone marrow (and, to a lesser extent, in the blood) lie millions and millions of stem cells. These are the "mother cells" from which all other blood cells form. The least developed type of stem cell is called "pluripotent." Pluripotent cells are probably as close as nature ever gets to immortality. They can produce identical copies of themselves, seemingly forever. As the copies mature, they change into every type of blood cell, including red cells, platelets, and the many different types of white cells. (See Table 2, page 152).

Because red cells live only four months or so,[23] the stem cells in the bone marrow must continuously make new ones. The manufacturing process uses some recycled materials and some fresh ones. Old red blood cells are broken down in the spleen and liver. The oxygen-carrying molecule hemoglobin contains iron. Some of the iron from dead red cells goes back to the bone marrow for recycling into new hemoglobin molecules; but some is lost, so a fresh supply is always needed from iron-rich foods.

Thanks to the bloodstream, beneficial drugs move from the site of an injection or from the stomach to all parts of the body. For example, an aspirin in the stomach breaks down into molecules small enough to pass through the walls of the small intestine and into the capillaries. Molecules then circulate in the bloodstream and move out through capillary walls in other places in the body.

A drug affects its target organ because of receptors on the surface of cells. Like a key that must fit a lock, the drug molecule has to fit a receptor; otherwise, it has no effect. Aspirin molecules relieve headache or muscle pain because they bind to receptor sites in the brain, blocking pain messages carried through nerves. When the molecule breaks down or falls away from the receptor site, the brain again receives pain signals, and it may be time for another dose.

About four weeks after egg and sperm unite and begin to develop in the uterus, an embryo's heart starts to beat. But the heart is not fully formed. It begins as a simple tube, then divides into two chambers—an atrium and a ventricle. About a week later, the heart adds a third chamber; now there are two partially separated atria and a single ventricle. By eight weeks, the heart has four separate chambers, with two separated ventricles.

Seven more months pass before the new heart and circulatory system can function independently of the mother. While growing and developing in the uterus, the fetus depends on the mother's blood to deliver food and oxygen and to carry away wastes. The mother's blood does not mix with her infant's. Instead, molecules of nutrients, water, oxygen, and waste pass back and forth through capillary walls in the placenta.

In an unborn child, pulmonary circulation is useless. The lungs are filled with fluid, and the fetus does not breathe. Most of the blood pumped into the pulmonary artery drains back into the aorta through a small tube. But all that changes at birth. The cutting of the umbilical cord and the first breath of air stop the exchange of materials across the placenta and set the gas-trading mechanisms of the lungs into motion.

The structure of the infant's circulatory system changes immediately. The tube that drained blood from the pulmonary artery back into the aorta closes. So does an opening between the two atria. In seconds, the dual closed loops of the adult circulatory system form and begin to function as separate systems.

How Does the Circulatory System Change Over Time?

You were born with all the heart cells you'll ever have. Your heart grows not because cells divide, but because they get bigger. At birth, your fist and your heart were about the same size, and that relationship continues throughout life.

The heart rate of a newborn averages 120 beats a minute. It slows to some 80 to 100 in childhood and settles at its adult rate of somewhere between 60 and 80 beats in the teens.[24] (Remember that these are averages. Your rate may vary from this figure and still be normal.)

From birth to about age five, the red marrow of virtually all the bones makes red blood cells. (The other marrow is yellow and mostly fat, but it can become red marrow when the body needs more red cells.) Between ages five and 20, the long bones gradually lose their production capacity. After age 20, most red cells are made in the marrow of the vertebrae (small bones of the back), sternum (breastbone), ribs, and pelvis.

In a newborn, the blood's clotting ability is only 40 or 45 percent of what it will become in early childhood. From that time on, it stays the same into the teen years, then starts to increase again during adult life. In the elderly, clotting capacity can reach almost twice what it was in the young adult.[25]

Although we usually think of heart disease as a killer of middle-aged and elderly people, the clogging of arteries with fatty deposits called plaque begins in childhood. Arteries begin to stiffen and harden in the teen years.

St. Valentine Gets a Chemistry Lesson

· · · · ·

Romance—long the domain of poets, philosophers and five-hankie movies—may be ruled as much by molecules as by emotion.

NUNA ALBERTS

· · · · ·

With trembling fingers, you ease open the envelope and withdraw the card inside. Your palms sweat. Butterflies dance in your stomach. Although your heart is pounding and your face feels hot, your tingling feet seem to walk on air. Are you coming down with a virus? No. It's St. Valentine's Day, and you're in love! (And from the words on the card, you know that special someone returns the sentiment!)

Every year on February 14, people in the United States, Canada, Mexico, Great Britain, France, and Australia celebrate Valentine's Day.

The practice of sending cards dates back to the fifteenth century, but the holiday itself is much older.

The Romans celebrated the festival of Lupercalia on February 15, back when February fell in early spring. On that day, crowds of people gathered in caves for the sacrifice of a dog or goat. They then cut the hide of the animal into long strips, dipped the strips in blood, and ran through the streets hitting people with them. (Hey, it was a pagan festival!) Women eager to bear children longed to be swatted with the strips, believing their fertility would increase. In the evening,

teenagers drew names and "went steady" for the following year. Lupercalia eventually led to Valentine's Day, but not until a Roman emperor got into the act.

In A.D. 269 or 270 (calendars were a bit quirky then), Emperor Claudius II—also called Claudius the Cruel—noticed that married men would rather stay home with their families than march off to war. Claudius thought he could hold onto his armies better if he forbade his soldiers to marry. But there's always someone around who'll buck authority. Legend has it that a Christian priest named Valentine married soldiers and their sweethearts in secret. Claudius found out about Valentine and threw him in prison.

Not one to give up on love, Valentine fell head over heels for the jailer's blind daughter. Just before Claudius had him beheaded, Valentine sent a love note to the girl signed "From your Valentine." It is said that he enclosed a crocus and that the girl recovered her vision on the day of Valentine's execution.

Two centuries later, the Christian church got rid of Lupercalia by substituting Valentine's Day. Since February 14 was believed to be both the day of Valentine's execution and the day that lovebirds select their lifemates, the shift in date was easy. Today, Americans give 40 million roses on that day and send 900 million Valentine cards, according to the Greeting Card Association.

For St. Valentine and for all those who have made, bought, sent, or received Valentine cards, love is a mysterious, elusive, wondrous miracle. Or is it? No matter what St. Valentine may have thought, scientists today generally agree that love is more a matter of chemistry than charisma.[26]

Hormones are proteins that circulate in the blood. Secreted by one organ, they influence another. Neurotransmitters are proteins that carry messages between nerve cells. They are extremely important in the brain. Modern scientists say that surges of hormones and neurotransmitters produce the various feelings we associate with love.

That meeting of gazes across a crowded room, for example, results from testosterone, the male hormone. Also present in females, albeit in smaller quantities, testosterone makes sure strangers don't stay strangers long. The physical effects of that initial attraction range from a sinking feeling in the stomach to flushed cheeks, sweaty palms, and loss of appetite.

The brain gets into the act, too. Spot a person you find attractive, and a part of the hypothalamus in the brain releases the neurotransmitter dopamine. Dopamine, in turn, triggers the brain's emotional responses. The heart pounds. Pupils widen. Skin glows as blood rushes to the face. The hair even becomes shinier because glands in the scalp produce extra oil.

After that first attraction, comes the feeling of being "in love." "When you are infatuated," says Rutgers University anthropologist Helen Fisher, "various chemicals, including dopamine, are released in your brain that work very much like amphetamines. . . . Lovers have all that energy—they can stay awake all night without feeling the least bit tired the next day, they lose weight, they feel optimistic, giddy, and full of life. They're high on natural speed."[27] Fisher points out that dopamine is known to be associated with "euphoria, sleeplessness, loss of appetite, and a rush of motivation."[28]

Other brain chemicals get into the act, especially phenylethylamine (PEA). PEA is also present in chocolate, which may explain why a box of candy makes such a dandy Valentine's Day present. Norepinephrine levels also increase, so that you get "high" on a cocktail of your own brain chemicals. But don't expect this phase of love to last. Perhaps the level of neurotransmitters drops after a while; or maybe nerve endings in the brain lessen their response to them. In either case, being "in love" typically lasts somewhere between 18 months and three years.

Then it's either break-up time—when the couple end their relationship and move on to seek a fresh neurotransmitter "fix"—or they make a long-term commitment.

Lasting love or attachment develops after infatuation fades. The thrill of love disappears, to be replaced by warm, secure feelings of safety and contentment (for those lucky in love, anyway). Attachment depends partly on the hormone oxytocin produced in the hypothalamus. That same hormone floods the bloodstream of a new mother. It prompts her to fall madly in love with her baby. Men make it too, but in smaller quantities. Evidence suggests that oxytocin strengthens emotional responses and makes memories of the loved one easier to retrieve while apart.

Long-term relationships also boost levels of brain chemicals called endorphins. Endorphins are the body's natural painkillers. They produce feelings of peace, contentment, and well being. Although proof is lacking, some scientists speculate that time spent with friends and lovers boosts endorphin levels. When separated, endorphin levels fall, and we find ourselves missing those significant others.

The chemicals of love affect all body systems, most noticeably the heart and circulation. Love makes the heart pound in the chest. Pulse rate increases. Blood pressure rises. It's no wonder that the ancients considered the heart, not the brain, the seat of love and emotion. Experts compare the chemistry of love with the rush of physical changes that prepares us to battle or to run from a wild animal on the attack. "It's the fight-or-flight mechanism, except you don't want to fight or flee," says Anthony Walsh, author of *The Science of Love*.[29]

Does all this scientific analysis rob love of its mystery and excitement? Pauline Williamson answers that question in her delightful poem. . . .

"Hormones"

Since Adam and Eve
at the 'ginin of time
we've had some feelins
that we just can't deny
it has nothin to do
with love and romance
when you move to the beat
of the primal dance
feel the fire rushin up ya
and tinglin your skin
you feel it all buildin from deep within
when you have to ask
is this love or this lust
just put your faith
in someone you can trust
when your body's just sayin
you gotta have that
and your heart doesn't care
who's holdin the bat
then the bug that you've got
is a chemical stew
so just go and enjoy it
you know that I do!

• • • • •

CHAPTER TWO

15
QUESTIONS
ABOUT THE HEART

Doctors call it a pump; poets call it a place where
love lives—or dies. [The truth] must lie somewhere between.

• EDNA BUCHANAN •

What Is Blood Pressure, and Why Is It Two Numbers?

Blood pressure might better be called heart pressure, for the heart's pumping action creates it. To measure blood pressure, health workers determine how hard the blood is pushing at two different times: when the heart contracts, called systole; and when the heart relaxes, called diastole.

The contraction of the ventricles during systole gives the blood a strong push, like the rush of water through a hose when the spigot is turned on. The force propels the blood through the arteries; it also pushes against artery walls. The first number in a blood pressure reading is the systole number. It is a larger number because the

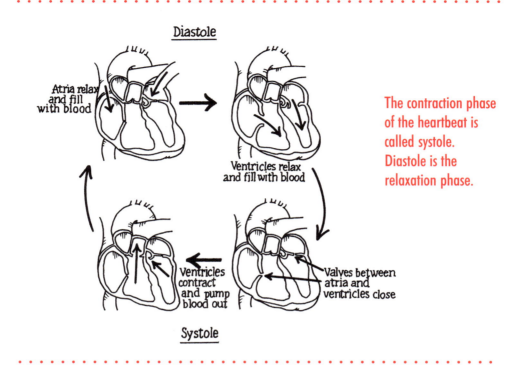

Diastole

Atria relax and fill with blood

Ventricles relax and fill with blood

Ventricles contract and pump blood out

Valves between atria and ventricles close

Systole

The contraction phase of the heartbeat is called systole. Diastole is the relaxation phase.

pressure of blood against artery walls is greater with the push of the heart's contraction behind it.

Diastole is the relaxation phase of heartbeat. Pressure diminishes within the relaxing ventricles. The pressure that blood exerts on artery walls decreases, too. This is the second number in a blood pressure measurement. It is always smaller than the first.

Blood pressure is not the same in all parts of the body, so to make comparisons meaningful, blood pressure is usually measured in the main artery of the upper arm. Also, blood pressure increases with exercise, stress, or exertion, so its readings are most accurate when the subject is lying down and relaxed.

Blood pressure is measured in millimeters of mercury. The blood pressure of a healthy adult might be recorded as 115/70 (read one-fifteen over seventy.) The normal range is about 100 to 120 systolic pressure and 60 to 80 diastolic. Doctors may diagnose high blood pressure, also called hypertension, when systole persistently exceeds 140 and diastole tops 90.

Is My Heartbeat the Sound of My Heart Contracting?

Doctors say the heart makes two sounds when it beats. They call the sounds "lub, dub." These are not the sounds of contraction, but the sounds made by the valves as they close between the chambers of the heart.

During systole, the valves close between the atria and the ventricles. They prevent backflow from ventricles to the atria. At the same time, the valves to the arteries—both pulmonary and aorta—open. This makes the first "lub" sound.

During diastole, the opposite occurs. The valves between the ventricles and the arteries shut, while those between the atria and ventricles open. This makes the "dub" sound.

Sometimes I Can Feel My Heart in My Stomach or Feel It Skip a Beat. Are Those Things Normal?

Usually, yes. When the heart contracts, it sends a surge of blood into the large arteries. Arteries are stretchy. They expand with that surge, then relax between heartbeats. In your stomach, arteries lie close enough to the skin surface that you can feel the expansion and relaxation a fraction of a second after the heart beats. You have similar "pulse points" at your thumb, wrist, and temple and behind your knee.

You can feel your heart pound when you are excited or frightened. Epinephrine, the "fight-or-flight" hormone from the adrenal glands, causes that. Exercise accelerates the heart, and fear, illness, excitement, or drugs can cause a pounding in the chest. Doctors call the sensation of a skipped beat PVC (for premature ventricular contraction). It is both common and harmless.

However, some irregular speeds or rhythms are not normal. Frequent episodes of irregular beating accompanied by breathlessness or dizziness require medical attention. So does a heart that consistently beats too rapidly. The most serious of the heart's irregular rhythms is called ventricular fibrillation. It is the rapid, shallow, and ineffective contraction of the ventricles.

Does My Heart Get Tired and Need Rest?

Never. Beating on the average 72 times a minute, your heart circulates about five liters a minute or more than 2,000 gallons a day[1]—and that's if you're a dedicated couch potato! Get up and going and your heart can move as much as eight gallons (30 liters) of blood a minute.[2] All this for as long as you live—about 2.5 billion beats in a lifetime!—and the heart never once takes a break.

What Is an ECG or EKG?

The letters stand for *electro*cardiogram or *electro*kardiogram. Either abbreviation means the same thing: a test of the heart's electrical

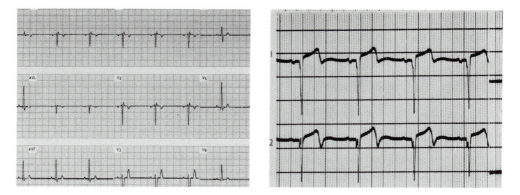

Patterns of electrical activity during a normal ECG, on the left, and an ECG recording of a patient's heart during a heart attack.

activity. Electrodes attached to the chest, abdomen, and back pick up electrical signals from the heart. Wires carry impulses to the electrocardiograph machine, which records them as a series of peaks and valleys. The lines on the graph can reveal either normal or abnormal heart functions.

ECGs are often recorded while the subject exercises on a treadmill or pedals a stationary bicycle. That's because exertion can trigger irregularities in the heart's electrical output that don't occur at rest. Most ECG readings are taken in the doctor's office or hospital laboratory, but patients who need round-the-clock surveillance may wear a Holter monitor. This miniature ECG machine hides under clothing and works while the patient goes about normal daily activities.

What's a Pacemaker, and Why Do Some People Have to Get One?

There are actually two kinds of pacemakers: the natural ones we are born with, and the electronic ones we may need later in life.

The heart's natural pacemaker, also called the sinoatrial or S-A node, is a bundle of nerve and muscle tissue in the right atrium. These cells differ from other heart muscle cells. They contract on their own, without any signal or stimulus from other cells.

The S-A node sends out a tiny electrical impulse that travels through the muscular walls of the atria. The impulse travels to the atrioventricular or A-V node, located between the atria and the ventricles. From there, it continues through the muscular walls of the ventricles, causing them to contract. The pacemaker keeps all parts of the heart working together, so that the pumping action is efficient and flawless.

Two nerves—the vagus and the sympathetic—deliver signals from the brain to the pacemaker. Vagus impulses slow heart rate; sympathetic impulses accelerate it. Pacemaker cells work by opening channels in cell membranes, where charged atoms of sodium and potassium move in and out of the cell. "A pacemaker channel senses that a cell has just fired [released an electrical impulse] and tells it that it can't rest, it has to fire another," explains Steven Siegelbaum of Columbia University.

Chemicals—either natural or introduced—can speed or slow the action of pacemaker cells. One example of a natural chemical effect is the hormone epinephrine. In times of stress, it makes the pacemaker fire rapidly, speeding up the heart and increasing the supply of nutrients and oxygen to muscles. The caffeine in coffee and the nicotine in cigarettes have the same effect.

Only when the natural pacemaker fails must an artificial one be implanted. Modern electronic pacemakers are small enough to fit inside the chest. They speed a slow heartbeat or even out an irregular one. Generally, two parts work together in an artificial pacemaker. A generator uses battery power to initiate electrical impulses that start the heartbeat. Tiny wires connect it to the heart. The second part is a sensing device that measures heart rate. When the heart rate is too slow, the sensor triggers the generator to send more impulses. When the heart beats too fast, the sensor turns off the generator.

How Does the Heart Muscle Contract? Membranes surround each heart muscle cell. Proteins on the membrane carry both signals and materials into and out of the cell. Think of these proteins as pumps so tiny that they work on a molecular scale. The pumps push positive and negative ions (charged atoms) across the cell's outer membrane. Other proteins act as floodgates. When they open, ions rush in. Changes in these ions—their amounts, their charges, and their locations—trigger or inhibit the contraction of proteins inside the cell.

When the heart rests, as it does for a fraction of a second between beats, the inside of the cell has a negative charge compared to the outside. But a signal from the heart's natural pacemaker briefly decreases the difference. The floodgates open, and positively charged sodium atoms surge inside. That change in charge causes the floodgates for charged ions of calcium to open. When calcium ions gather around contractile proteins inside the cell, the cell shortens and thickens.

With millions of heart cells acting in the same way, the result is the push of blood we hear as a heartbeat and feel as a pulse. The cells return to their resting state because the pumps push sodium and calcium out of the cell and return it to its slightly negatively charged state.

Can Stress Affect Blood Pressure? "In these days of 70 hour work weeks, pagers, fax machines, and endless committee meetings, stress has become a prevalent part of people's lives," writes Shveta Kulkarni and her colleagues at the Medical College of Wisconsin.[3] Whenever you're stressed, your blood pressure rises temporarily. That's because the nervous system produces chemicals that narrow blood vessels. (Imagine water forced from a larger pipe into a smaller one. The pressure in the smaller pipe is higher.) Most of the time, pressure soon drops to normal, and no long-term ill effects result. However, if pressure rises and stays high (hypertension), the risk of heart attacks and strokes increases. Kulkarni says stress isn't the direct cause of high blood pressure, but a contributor to its development over time. Stress factors that affect blood pressure include work problems, race, social environment, and emotional distress.

Why Do I Get Light-headed When I Stand Up Quickly?

Standing quickly leaves blood pooled in your legs. Blood pressure drops, and for an instant the brain gets too little blood. A second or two passes before your nervous system can trigger the release of the hormone epinephrine from your pancreas. As soon as epinephrine takes effect, the heart beats a little faster and blood pressure rises. That increases the flow of blood to your brain, and you feel normal again.

Is Heartburn Really a Heart Burn?

The next time you feel that burning sensation in your chest, don't call it heartburn, call it GERD. GERD—for *gastroesophageal reflux disease*—is a burning pain, all right, but it has nothing to do with your heart. The burning sensation happens when acid from the stomach moves up into the esophagus (the food tube between throat and stomach) and irritates its lining. GERD comes after eating, and may be accompanied by burping and bad tastes. Over-the-counter antacids can handle an occasional bout of GERD. Frequent or persistent cases need a doctor's attention.

What's a Heart Murmur?

A healthy heart beats with a steady lub, dub sound. Whispers, swishes, and whooshing sounds—or "murmurs"—can sometimes result from nothing more than the rush of the blood through the heart. Or a more serious malfunction may be the cause.

Leaky valves or incomplete closures between heart chambers can cause murmurs. Often, doctors can tell from heart sounds if blood is backing up into a ventricle rather than flowing into an artery. They can also determine if a defect in the wall that divides the sides of the heart is permitting mixing of blood between the right and left sides.

Sometimes a "blowing" sound indicates a weak spot in an artery wall. A "swishing" sound may reveal a leaky valve. A "clicking" sound may betray a defect in the mitral valve between the left atrium and left ventricle.

How Does Drug Abuse Affect the Heart?

Scientists can't answer that question fully, but some effects are known. For example, cocaine increases the risk of heart attack by a factor of 24 within the first hour after its use.[4] The drug attacks cells that line the inner walls of blood vessels. It makes them release a chemical that causes them to contract. The contraction raises blood pressure and chokes off blood supply to the heart.

Marijuana is another drug that affects the heart and circulation in several ways. It dilates capillaries, making the whites of the eyes look bloodshot. It also increases heart rate. If the more rapid heartbeat is not enough to maintain blood flow, clots can form in small arteries that supply blood to vital organs such as the kidneys. Damage to the organ or loss of function results. Marijuana also interferes with the body's temperature controls. In the first hour after use, smoking marijuana multiplies by five the risk of a heart attack.[5]

A few other known effects of drugs include the following:

- Injecting drugs such as heroin into the veins can lead to infections of the heart or blood vessels. Such infections can provoke heart failure, heart attack, or stroke.

- Substances, such as talc, used to "cut" drugs may fail to dissolve in the bloodstream. They can block blood flow in narrow vessels causing heart attack or stroke.

- Cocaine and inhaled drugs can cause the heart to beat with an abnormal rhythm.

- Heroin and other drugs derived from opium can interfere with gas exchange in the lungs.

- Drugs that induce hallucinations, such as PCP ("angel dust") or LSD, can rupture blood vessels in the brain and cause both heart and lungs to shut down.

- Stimulant drugs, such as amphetamines ("speed"), accelerate breathing and heart rate and elevate blood pressure.

Not all drugs that affect the heart are illegal. Alcohol raises blood levels of triglycerides, a form of fat associated with heart disease. Too much alcohol can raise blood pressure and trigger heart failure. Heavy use of alcohol over time induces loss of heart muscle tissue. Large doses of alcohol can interfere with the blood supply to the brain, causing a stroke. Smoking a cigarette increases blood pressure and heart rate. It decreases blood flow to the fingers and toes which, over time, can cause serious circulatory disorders of the limbs. Tobacco raises the level of carbon monoxide in the blood. Along with nicotine, that compound increases the risk of heart disease and heart attack.

Can the Mind Control Blood Pressure or Heart Rate?

Whether it's meditation, acupressure, biofeedback, yoga, hypnosis, massage, mental imagery, or music, "mind-over-matter" techniques work—for *some* of the people *some* of the time.

One famous study in Oakland, California, for example, looked at mildly elevated blood pressure in elderly African-Americans. All subjects received advice to exercise, eat right, and stop smoking. In addition, some of the participants learned transcendental meditation. By uttering a word repeatedly, they entered a trance-like state that relaxes the body and slows the heart. Another group learned a method of relaxing muscles. After three months, the people who meditated had lower blood pressure than the controls who worked only on their lifestyles. The muscle relaxation group improved, too, although not as much as those who meditated.

Biofeedback is another way of learning to control "involuntary" body processes. People who learn biofeedback hook up to computers set to measure blood pressure, heart rate, or some other variable. The subject concentrates on achieving a goal, such as slowing the heart or relaxing arteries. When progress is made, sounds or lights signal success. Gradually, new goals are set and achieved, and some subjects can eventually lower or moderate their heart rate or blood pressure without the aid of the computer. Biofeedback is both controversial and difficult to study. While success stories are many, hard data are scarce.

Perhaps mental focus is the key. Researchers in Los Angeles studied 210 people who had at least one risk factor for heart disease, such as high cholesterol (a fat in the blood) or a smoking habit. They showed half the people an ultrasound picture of their clogged carotid artery, but didn't give them a picture to take home. They gave the other half of the people copies of the picture to carry in their wallets and post on their refrigerators. After six months, those who took the pictures home with them were more likely to have lost weight or quit smoking. Twice as many of them started exercising.[6]

How Are Heart Transplants Done, and How Common Are They?

In hospitals all over the world, heart transplants have become common, if not routine, procedures. Somewhere a heart donor has died, probably in an accident. Somewhere else, a heart patient's phone rings. "We've found a donor for you," a doctor says, ending a wait that may have lasted months, even years.

On the donor's end, doctors have declared death. Brain waves have stopped, although the heart still beats. A surgical team opens the chest, inspects the heart, and performs tests to make sure the heart is healthy. If it is pronounced disease-free, the surgeon uses a chemical solution to stop its contraction. Its connections to arteries and veins are severed. The heart is cooled to preserve it during its rush trip to another hospital. It can last only four to six hours,[7] so swift action is required.

At the recipient's hospital, the patient is prepared for surgery. The chest cavity is opened, and the patient's circulation is transferred to a heart/lung machine. The patient's heart is cut away at the aorta, pulmonary artery, and left and right atria. Then those connections are reestablished to those of the donor heart.

Today, more than 2,000 heart transplants are performed annually in the United States alone. Four out of every five heart recipients survive for a year; three in four survive for three years.[8] The major obstacle to increasing the number of transplants is a shortage of donors. Too few hearts are available for the many thousands who need and want them.

As this graph shows, nearly half of all heart transplant recipients survive for ten years or more.

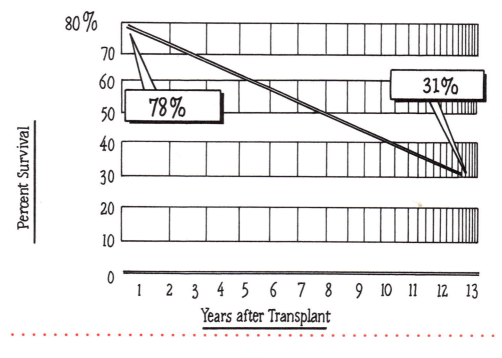

The answer depends on the animal. The hearts of less-advanced animals are usually simpler, and they pump blood in open systems with few or no vessels. (Only a few animals without backbones have closed systems.) In insects, for example, the pump is a muscular tube, more like a blood vessel than a human heart. It pushes blood into the open spaces of the body cavity, where it bathes the internal organs with food and oxygen. Other tubes collect the blood from the spaces and return it, along with its load of wastes, to the pumping vessel. This system works only because insects have many openings in their bodies that let in air, so gases can be exchanged directly.

Mammals and birds have four-chambered hearts. Many other animals do quite well with simpler designs.

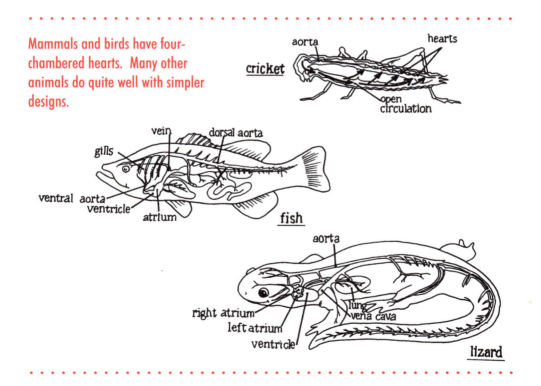

aorta   hearts

cricket

open circulation

vein   dorsal aorta

gills

ventral aorta
ventricle
atrium

fish

aorta

right atrium
left atrium
ventricle

lung
vena cava

lizard

All mammals (including humans) and birds have a heart with four chambers. Oxygen-rich and oxygen-poor blood are completely separated on the two sides. Amphibians, such as the frog, have two atria that separate oxygenated and deoxygenated blood, but blood mixes in a single ventricle. Some of the blood leaving the ventricle travels to the lungs; the rest goes to the body. Some lizards and snakes have partially separated ventricles, while others have four-chambered hearts similar to those of mammals and birds. Fish have simple hearts with two chambers, one atrium and one ventricle. The ventricle pumps blood to the gills which, like lungs in higher animals, handle the exchange of gases with the environment (in this case water, not air). All animals with backbones—whether fish, amphibians, reptiles, or birds—have a closed system of blood vessels.

Some animals, such as pigs, have hearts that are so much like humans' that their valves can be removed, preserved, and used to replace diseased ones in people. The pericardium, the sac that surrounds the heart, can be taken from cows and used to make artificial aortic valves. These tissue valves are being used more and more. Some last as long as ten or 15 years. [9]

Trailing the TAH

· · · · ·

Thanks to the human heart by which we live.

WILLIAM WORDSWORTH

· · · · ·

An engineer's specifications for the human heart might read like this:

- lightweight
- portable
- cheap
- no corrosion, breakdown, or maintenance
- no rough edge or corners
- acceleration/deceleration without external control
- dual—separate but coordinated—pumping systems
- four valves, coordinated function—no backflow, leakage, or mixing.

As tall as that order seems, it's precisely what inventors must deliver if the dream of a Totally Artificial Heart—TAH, for short—is ever to become reality. No machine has yet done everything the human heart can do—at least not for very long. Still, research has come a long way, and mechanical devices are routinely assisting or partially replacing diseased and disabled human hearts.

One example is replacement of the valves of the heart damaged by infections, age, or birth defects. One in every 300 children is born with a faulty valve.[10] Any malfunction of a valve makes the heart work harder or even fail. Minor defects in valves can be repaired using the patient's own tissues. Major abnormalities require replacement with a human, animal, or mechanical valve.

Mechanical valves work just like natural heart valves. Rising pressure on one side of the valve causes it to open. As blood passes through, pressure builds on the other side, and the valve closes. The first mechanical valve was put into a patient in 1961. By 1996, nearly 80,000 valve replacement procedures were being performed in the United States annually.[11]

Devices that partially support a failing heart are in common use as well. For example, many hospitals now implant LVADs (*l*eft *v*entricular *a*ssist *d*evice). This air-driven pump receives blood from the left ventricle and gives it an extra push into the aorta. The air flows from an external computer-controlled console through a tube in the patient's abdomen. In use since the 1950s, temporary LVADs act as stopgap measures to assist a failing heart while a patient waits for a transplant. Although hooked to a large battery-powered console, the patient can move around and exercise.

Sometimes an LVAD is more than a bridge to transplantation. Sometimes, it can be a cure in itself. Nearly five million Americans suffer from heart failure.[12] Their hearts contract weakly, relax slowly, and fail to respond to hormones that

speed up a normal heart. Given LVAD's assistance and a chance to heal, the damaged cells of a failing heart can sometimes recover their contracting power. Some people improve so much that they can cancel their transplants.

LVADs are used in hospitals, but one famous heart surgeon hopes to send them home. Michael DeBakey, who implanted the first VAD in a human in 1966, has teamed up with researchers at NASA to develop a new kind of VAD. It's about the size of a fountain pen, small enough to implant in children. Its size also means it can be placed in the chest and powered by a battery pack worn on the belt. Despite its size, it's powerful enough to increase blood flow up to ten liters (about ten quarts) a minute. DeBakey's VAD has only one moving part, which researchers hope will minimize risks of damaging red cells and clotting. It could never provide a permanent solution, but it might allow a patient to leave the hospital while waiting for a transplant.

LVADs are valuable, but they fall short of meeting the engineer's list of criteria for a TAH. Not that TAHs haven't been tried. In 1957, a team led by Dutch-born physician Willem

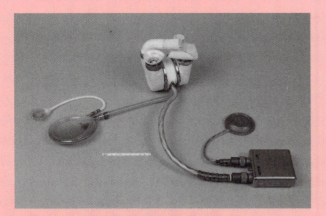

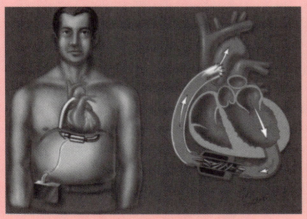

Kolff tested a model in animals. In 1969, Denton Cooley, at the Texas Heart Institute, kept a patient alive for more than 60 hours with a different model.

In 1982, Dr. William DeVries, of the University of Utah, implanted an artificial heart in Barney Clark, an elderly dentist too ill for a trans-plant. Clark survived for 112 days, tethered to an air cable mounted on a console the size of a washing machine. Later, other patients received improved models of this device, named the Jarvik heart, after its inventor. All died of complications such as clots or infections. One lived for nearly two years, but he suffered infections and fevers. His blood clotted, causing multiple strokes. Such tragic stories ended trials of the Jarvik heart.

In 1988, the National Heart, Lung, and Blood Institute revived the dream of a TAH by granting 23 million dollars to four contractors who wanted to try to build a working TAH. Ten years later, two candidates emerged with promising prototypes. Abiomed, a company in Cambridge, Massachusetts, developed a TAH they call PulsaCor. Its pump weighs less than two pounds. It has four valves like the human heart, but only two chambers. Batteries implanted in the abdomen power its electric motor. An external magnetic coil transmits power painlessly through the skin to a receiving coil under the skin.

Researchers at Pennsylvania State University have enjoyed similar success with their device. To measure durability, researchers at Penn State submerged their system in salt water. Maintained in large fish tanks at the same temperature as the human body, the TAH pumps water 24 hours a day, seven days a week. "The goal is to have all of the heart sys-

tems run for two years without any problems," says researcher Alan Snyder. That goal drew nearer in October, 1999, when the University's TAH was tested for the first time in a human patient—successfully!

What you are reading now is only an introduction to TAH. By the time you open this book, new chapters in the story will have been written. Search newspapers and magazines for up-to-date reports on TAHs. Are they being tried in animals? In humans? Have they failed or succeeded? Are engineers heading "back to the drawing board" to correct difficulties they failed to foresee?

One fact won't change: the need for a truly functional artificial heart is great. The American Heart Association estimates that 40,000 Americans age 65 or younger could benefit from a heart transplant each year, but fewer than 2,500 actually get one.[13] "When the body's major organ packs up, an artificial pump is the only solution," says Wilbert Keon, Director General of the Ottawa Heart Institute. "There will never be enough human hearts to transplant," he says.[14]

• • • • •

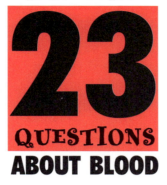

CHAPTER THREE

23

QUESTIONS

ABOUT BLOOD

The stream is blood; every drop is alive.
• RALPH WALDO EMERSON •

How Does My Blood Fight Disease?

Leukocytes are the body's primary disease fighters. They squeeze through the thin walls of capillaries out into the lymph. Lymph is the clear fluid that bathes every cell in the body. It circulates through a series of interconnected vessels, but the lymphatic system lacks the pumping action of the heart. It moves by gravity and muscle action. Lymph collects in nodes in the neck, groin, chest, abdomen, and armpits. Along with the spleen, these nodes act as filters, trapping disease-causing organisms and removing them from circulation. The cells that circulate in lymph return to the bloodstream through lymph vessels.

There are many different kinds of leukocytes. (For more detail, see Table 2, page 152.) Phagocytes ("eating cells") are one type. They capture and engulf microbes, digesting them with enzymes and absorbing their parts. Monocytes, the largest phagocytes, move with the blood, consuming any foreign invaders they come across. Macrophages are similar to monocytes, but they don't circulate. They reside among the cells they serve. They live up to their name of "big eater" by devouring any microbes that come their way.

Another important category of white blood cell is the lymphocytes. They are made in the bone marrow, liver, and spleen and set loose into the bloodstream. B cells are lymphocytes made in bone marrow. They are factories for the production of antibodies. Antibodies are proteins.

Two immune system cells — the long cell is a dendritic cell and the round one is a T cell.

They circulate in blood and latch onto invaders, marking them for destruction. The body can produce millions of different kinds of antibodies, each uniquely shaped to hook onto a single kind of disease-causing microbe.

T cells are another important kind of lymphocyte. When a T cell recognizes a foreign protein, helper T cells signal the B cells to start producing antibodies or to speed up production. Suppressor T cells slow or stop the manufacture of antibodies. Killer T cells demolish invaders by splitting their cell membranes with enzymes. They also obliterate body cells infected with viruses.

Neutrophils, the most numerous leukocytes in the blood, belong to a class of cells called granulocytes. All granulocytes are made in bone marrow. Their granules act as storage depots for infection-fighting chemicals. To release their chemical weapons, the granules fuse with the cell membrane. That opens the granule to the outside, and its contents spill out.

Yet another kind of leukocyte has a special job to do. Natural killer or NK cells secrete an enzyme that dissolves the membranes of cells that display foreign or abnormal proteins. Along with killer T cells, NK cells are powerful weapons against many cancer cells and cells infected with viruses.

Not all infection-fighters are cells or antibodies. Some 15 or more enzymes[1] —together called complement, or the complement series—work in both blood and lymph. Complement effects a series of chemical reactions, each dependent upon the one before it. Particular proteins or sugars from the cell walls of bacteria start the sequence rolling, like dominoes falling in a line. Once the chain reaction begins, complement enzymes (1) release chemicals that recruit immune cells to the site; (2) attach a protein "marker" or "flag" to an invader cell, which attracts phagocytes; or (3) destroy a microbe by poking holes in its membrane.

How Do Red Cells Carry Oxygen?

A chemical change gets the job done. Red cells contain a compound called hemoglobin. Hemoglobin is a protein that contains an iron atom. It's the pigment that gives red cells their color, and it makes up about one-third of the weight of the red cell.[2] When an oxygen molecule comes along, it quickly combines with the iron, changing hemoglobin to oxyhemoglobin. But the bond isn't very tight. Where oxygen supplies are low, oxyhemoglobin readily gives up its load. It turns oxygen over to the living cells it serves. Hemoglobin also combines with carbon dioxide, which is also easily released in the lungs.

A computer-generated model of hemoglobin.

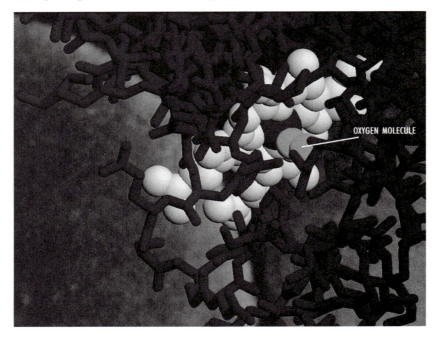

OXYGEN MOLECULE

Why Is Blood Red?

Have you ever noticed that blood smells metallic? The reason is the iron in hemoglobin, plus tiny amounts of copper, zinc, and other metals. When oxygen combines with hemoglobin, blood turns bright red. The deadly poison carbon monoxide gives it a cherry red hue. It binds to hemoglobin more tightly than either oxygen or carbon dioxide. Breathing the fumes from an automobile exhaust or faulty furnace can kill in minutes. The carbon monoxide locks to hemoglobin so tightly that the molecule cannot pick up or release other gases.

Is the Blood in My Veins Blue?

No, it's a dark, purplish red. Those blue vessels you see in your arm are veins. You are seeing not blood, but the fibrous walls of the veins as they look under a layer of skin. To a surgeon, they appear colorless. When you cut yourself and bleed from a vein, the blood looks bright red. Why? Because hemoglobin combines with oxygen as soon as it comes in contact with air.

Inside the body bright-red oxygen-rich blood flows through the arteries and the pulmonary vein. Dark-red blood that has lost its oxygen flows to the heart through veins and to the lungs through the pulmonary artery.

What's a Bruise, and Why Does It Change Color?

A bruise forms when a blood vessel breaks under the skin. Red blood cells leak out and lose their oxygen. The blood looks black or blue under the skin. As the hemoglobin breaks down, its chemical composition changes. It starts to look green or yellow before all its components are absorbed into surrounding cells and tissues or carried away by the lymph that flows around and between cells.

How Much Blood Do I Have in My Body?

The amount of blood you have depends on how big you are. On average, about 7 percent of your body weight is blood. If you weigh 150 pounds (68 kilograms), a little over ten pounds (5 kilograms) of you is blood. An average-size adult man has somewhere between five and seven quarts of blood (4.8 to 6.6 liters). Women generally have a little less than men, about four to six quarts (3.8 to 5.7 liters). But the ratios vary with age. Babies have more blood in relation to their body weight than adults do.[3]

How Far and How Fast Does Blood Travel around My Body?

If you could lay all your arteries, veins, and capillaries end to end, they would stretch over 60,000 miles (nearly 100,000 kilometers).[4] That's two and a half times around the world at the equator. Your heart is powerful enough to push blood into the aorta at a rate of about 15 inches (40 centimeters) per second.[5] Blood travels at speeds up to ten miles (16 kilometers) per hour.[6]

Does the Same Blood Travel to All Parts of the Body?

The same blood goes around repeatedly, but the destination of any individual blood cell is unpredictable. For example, the red cell that on one circuit carries oxygen to an arm muscle may serve the liver or inner ear on its next trip.

Do I Have the Same Blood Now That I Had Last Week?

No. In fact, it's not even the same as what you had a second ago. Ten million red cells die every second; 200 billion new ones form daily.[7] Your body continuously recycles blood's components and makes fresh cells.

What's a Hematocrit, and Why Do Doctors Measure It?

Place a blood sample in a test tube and spin it in a centrifuge for a while. (Imagine the spin cycle on a washing machine. That's how a centrifuge works.) The outward force of the spin pushes the heavier components of blood to the bottom of the tube. The lighter parts stay near the surface. The result is a series of layers, one atop the other, like oil-and-vinegar salad dressing that has separated.

At sea level, the hematocrit of a healthy adult man reads somewhere between 42 and 54 percent; a woman, 38 to 46 percent. A newborn's

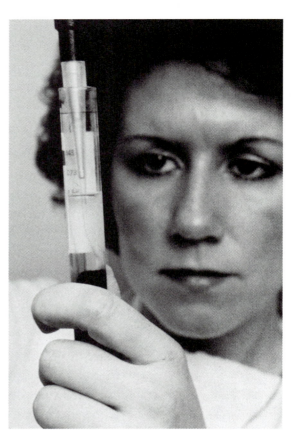

A hematocrit measures how much of the blood's volume is cells. When the blood is centrifuged, the plasma stays on top and the heavier red blood cells fall to the bottom.

normal values run much higher: 55 to 68 percent. These numbers represent the total volume of the red cells at the bottom of the tube *plus* the "buffy coat" of white cells and platelets lying just above. The plasma layer on top makes up the remaining (roughly) half. It is mostly water with blood proteins, nutrients, hormones, and electrolytes (ions) dissolved in it.

The volumes of the layers provide clues in diagnosing certain diseases. An elevated hematocrit may result from lung disease, heart failure, or cancer. Low values arise from anemia, internal bleeding, kidney disease, and hormonal disorders.

What Is Anemia, and How Is It Treated?

Anemia describes any condition in which the number of red cells in the blood is decreased or the blood's oxygen-carrying capacity is diminished. There are many types. For example:

- Aplastic: The bone marrow produces too few blood cells of all types.

- Hypoplastic: The bone marrow produces too few red cells.

- Autoimmune hemolytic: The immune system attacks and destroys blood cells.

- Hypochromic: Red cells contain too little hemoglobin.

- Iron deficiency: Without enough iron, the body cannot make enough hemoglobin or enough red cells.

- Idiopathic acquired hemolytic: Red cells don't live as long as they should.

- Microcytic: Red cells are too small.

- Pernicious: The body cannot absorb enough Vitamin B_{12}, which it needs to make hemoglobin.

The root cause for many types of anemia is unknown. We don't know why the body would destroy its own red cells or why the bone marrow should make too few. In other cases, the cause is known, and treatment can be directed accordingly. For example, eating more iron-rich vegetables or taking an iron supplement can reverse some forms of iron-deficiency anemia.

What Is Sickle-Cell Disease, and How Is It Treated?

Sickle-cell disease is perhaps the best-known of the inherited forms of anemia. It arises from the production of an abnormal hemoglobin molecule. The misshapen molecule causes the red cells to become misshapen, too, especially when oxygen levels are low. The bending of the cells into the characteristic sickle shape gives the disorder its name. The twisted cells tangle together and jam in capillaries. The tangles block blood flow, starve cells, and impede circulation. Jams of sickle cells in the heart or brain can be fatal.

In the United States, sickle-cell disease is the most common inherited disorder among African-Americans. It is inherited as a recessive. Usually, that means both parents—apparently normal and healthy themselves—carry the gene. The child who gets the genes from both parents (there's a one-in-four chance) has sickle-cell anemia. Fortunately, medical tests can now identify carriers and help parents plan their families.

Modern treatments also help relieve the symptoms of sickle-cell disease, which can vary greatly from one person to another. Analgesic drugs help those who experience severe pain. Exchange transfusions (exchange of the total blood volume) treat acute chest syndrome, a serious failure in lung function. Antibiotics fight infections. Doctors stay alert in case of strokes—most common among young children with sickle-cell disease—and declines in red blood cell production.

A bone-marrow transplant can cure sickle cell, replacing defective red cells with the donor's healthy ones. Unfortunately, such a transplant is impossible for most. Too few compatible donors are available, and the drugs required to prepare a patient for transplant are themselves risky.

What Is Hemophilia and How Is It Treated?

A series of proteins must interact and change to make blood clot. Any factor missing or defective anywhere in the series means a problem with clotting.

People with hemophilia are missing one or more of the clotting proteins or are making them in such small amounts that clotting is impaired. Fourteen (or perhaps more) different clotting factors have been named and numbered. People with hemophilia may suffer frequent or severe bruising and internal bleeding around the joints or in the body cavity.

Hemophilia A, or classic hemophilia, is inherited. About 85 percent of all hemophiliacs have this form. They are missing the clotting protein called Factor VIII (the Roman numeral for 8). A gene present on the X chromosome causes this form, so it nearly always affects males. Genes determine what proteins a cell will make. Boys with hemophilia A lack the gene that normally programs cells to make Factor VIII.

Hemophilia A is usually treated with periodic injections of Factor VIII, but some doctors hope that gene therapy will someday provide a permanent cure. Several different approaches offer promise. For example, researchers at the University of Pittsburgh have inserted normal Factor VIII genes into viruses that cannot reproduce themselves. When the virus "infects" cells in the liver and spleen, it should—in theory—set up Factor VIII "factories."

**What Happens
When the Body
Loses a Lot of
Blood?**

You probably know that losing a small amount of blood or donating a pint (about half a liter) produces few, if any, ill effects. The body speeds up production and replaces what is lost in hours or days.

But rapid loss of greater amounts triggers a chain reaction of problems. The decreasing volume of blood causes blood vessels to narrow. That limits the amount of oxygen that reaches body cells and tissues. Starved for oxygen, cells shift their pattern of energy use. Instead of combining glucose with oxygen to release the energy stored in food, cells switch to energy-releasing reactions that work without oxygen. This energy release keeps cells alive, but produces lactic acid as a waste product.

As its lactic-acid load increases, the blood's pH drops. (On the pH scale of 1–14, numbers below seven are acid. Numbers above seven are basic or alkaline.) Even a small shift toward acidity inhibits oxygen uptake and transport. Enzymes don't catalyze chemical reactions normally either. A pH that drops below 7.35 (just a little on the basic side of neutral) spells trouble, even death.

At the same time, the body tries to compensate for blood loss. The nervous system signals certain glands to increase their production of epinephrine, the hormone that speeds heart rate and elevates blood pressure. Other hormones surge into the bloodstream. They constrict blood vessels and cause the body to retain water and sodium. If blood loss is not too great, the body may be able to stabilize itself this way.

If it can't, the signs of shock may appear. Shock is a general term for the failure of the heart and blood vessels to supply blood to body tissues. Shock can arise from any of several different causes. Heart failure is an obvious one. Serious burns accompanied by a rapid loss of fluids can bring on shock, as can heavy bleeding or declining blood pressure.

The symptoms of shock include weakness, pallor, nausea, and thirst. The skin may feel cold and damp. In severe cases, the shock victim loses consciousness. Shock is treated with fluids, oxygen, and, when necessary, blood transfusions.

The loss of as little as a pint (half a liter) of blood can induce shock,[8] but it's possible to lose far greater amounts of blood and still survive, if medical treatment is swift and aggressive. Doctors define massive transfusions as replacement of the total volume of blood in less than 24 hours or more than half in an hour. In cases of severe bleeding, a patient may receive blood and fluids through high volume devices that deliver between 400 and 700 milliliters a minute. (For comparison, an ordinary can of soda contains 355 milliliters.)

What Is Blood Sugar, and What Regulates Its Level?

Glucose, a simple sugar, is fuel for living cells. The strong bonds between its carbon, hydrogen, and oxygen atoms store energy. When those bonds are broken, energy is released. The cells trap that energy in the bonds of other molecules and use it to power life functions.

Maintaining the right levels of glucose in blood and cells is a life-sustaining function. The hormone insulin, made in the pancreas, handles the job. It acts on the liver, muscle, and fatty tissues. It works by binding to sites on cell membranes. It opens "gates" in the membranes that let glucose molecules enter the cells. If too little insulin is made—or if the cells fail to open their gates in response to insulin—cells "starve." (It's significant that the movement of glucose into the brain, red blood cells, and liver does *not* depend on insulin.)

By moving glucose into cells at the proper rate, insulin maintains an

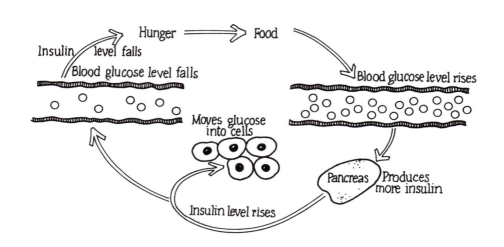

The control of blood sugar levels by the hormone insulin is a self-regulating system scientists call a feedback loop.

optimum concentration of sugar in the blood. After a meal, levels of blood sugar rise. In response, the pancreas releases more insulin. Increased levels of insulin cause more glucose to move into cells, where it is either used as energy (if needed immediately) or stored as fat (for use later). That returns the level of sugar in the blood to normal.

Insulin lasts only minutes in the blood, and it is broken down quickly by the liver and kidneys. Therefore, its level drops as blood sugar decreases, and less new insulin is made. If blood sugar levels drop too low, the liver changes some of its glycogen stores into glucose, which enters the blood and brings sugar levels up again. If glycogen stores are depleted or blood sugar levels dip even lower, the brain gets into the act.

You feel hungry.

Diabetes is a general term for a defect in this sugar-regulating system. Type I is inherited and usually appears in childhood or adolescence. The pancreas makes too little insulin, and pills or shots must supply it. Type II diabetes typically appears after age 40. The body produces enough insulin, but cells fail to respond to it. This type can usually be controlled with diet and exercise.

What Are Blood Types, and Why Are They Important?

If your medical report reads *A, Rh+, M, s, P1, Lua, K+, Kp(a-b+), Le(a-b+), Fy(a+), Jk(a+b+)*, don't run for a foreign-language dictionary. The letters aren't Greek. They are simply the names given to various proteins that may be present on the membranes of your blood cells. The proteins are grouped under names such as the Lutheran, Kell, Lewis, Duffy, and Kidd systems.

The most familiar blood proteins—and the first to be typed—are today known as the A–B–O blood groups. People with type A blood have the A protein (also called antigen) in their blood, but not the B. Type B blood means the B protein is present, but not the A. If both proteins occur, the type is called AB. Type O means neither protein is present.

Another well-known blood protein is named Rh. If you are Rh+ (read, R H positive), you have the protein. Rh- (read, R H negative) means you don't.

In most cases, the presence or absence of these antigens means nothing in terms of health. The types are simply differences among healthy people. There are, however, exceptions. For example, it's not likely that you are missing both of the Duffy system proteins, Fy a and Fy b, *unless* you live in a country where malaria is common. In such countries, many more people have the Fy(a-b-) Duffy type. They enjoy a certain degree of immunity against malaria that people who are positive for either protein lack. Why? Because the organism that causes malaria, *Plasmodium falciparum*, uses the Duffy antigens to enter red blood cells. Without them, the malarial parasite cannot infect.

The Rh factor becomes very important when an Rh- mother carries an Rh+ fetus. The first pregnancy is usually fine, but if any blood leaks through the placenta when the infant is born, the mother's blood may begin manufacturing anti-Rh antibodies. In her next pregnancy, her antibodies may attack and destroy cells in the baby's blood. A substance called RhoGAM given to the mother before her first delivery and shortly thereafter stops her body from making anti-Rh antibodies.

When and Why Is Blood Typing Done?

Fans of the popular television show *ER* know how important blood type is in an emergency. "Start the O-neg," shouts Dr. Green, and the team swings into action. Green calls for type O, Rh-negative blood in life-and-death situations when there's no time for blood-typing. Since that type contains no A, B, or Rh antigens, it can—in theory—be safely given to all.

The blood carries antibodies against the antigens that are *not* its own. Antibodies are defenses of the immune system. They destroy proteins the body recognizes as foreign. For example, if you have type A blood, you carry no antibodies against the A antigen, but your blood makes antibodies against the B antigen. Receive a type-B or type-AB transfusion, and your own blood will attack the B antigens in the donation. The locking of antibody to antigen causes cells to rupture and clump. Circulating clumps of red cells are a life-threatening emergency in themselves.

People with type AB blood carry both antigens and neither antibody. They can receive blood from any other type but can donate only to their own type. People with type O negative blood make no A, B, or Rh antigens, so they can give blood to all other types without fear of dangerous clumping. (The number of anti-A and anti-B antibodies in their blood is small and will do little harm in the recipient.)

In real life, O-negative is given far less often than television dramas might lead you to believe. For one thing, blood-typing can be done in minutes. For another, transfusing blood matched to the patient's own type is far safer than giving O-negative to everyone.

Do People Who Live At High Altitudes Have More Blood or Thicker Blood?

Suppose you move from New Orleans to Denver. In the Mile High City, atmospheric pressure is lower than at sea level, so each breath of air you take in contains fewer oxygen molecules. Your lungs cannot provide your red blood cells with as much oxygen as they did in New Orleans. Or, looking at the situation differently, your blood, acclimated to the Louisiana lowlands, contains too few red cells to capture enough oxygen in Denver's "thin" air. You can tell the difference. In the first days after your move, you feel a bit dizzy and lightheaded. But soon something happens that you are not aware of. Your kidneys (believe it or not!) detect low levels of oxygen in the blood. They respond by releasing a hormone that travels to the bone marrow and stimulates it to make more red cells. The normal count of red cells for people at sea level runs between 3.6 and 5.4 million cells per milliliter. People who live above 4,500 feet (about 1,400 meters) average 8 million or more.[9] People who live in the Andes at 10,000 feet (about 3,000 meters) or higher have larger lungs, more highly branched capillary beds, and faster average heart rates. Their blood contains 30 percent more red cells than people who live at sea level.

What Is Blood Poisoning?

Blood poisoning, or septicemia, is a bacterial infection in the blood that spreads throughout the body. It usually begins with a local infection that the body's immune system cannot contain. Symptoms include chills, fever, and fatigue. Large doses of antibiotics can often destroy the bacteria and restore health.

Do Adults Ever Grow New Blood Vessels?

Yes, but rarely. The body can form new capillary beds when a deep wound heals or during pregnancy. Sometimes a damaged heart even helps heal itself.

Doctors have long wondered why some heart patients can grow new blood vessels in the heart while others cannot. A team of researchers in Israel believes they may have an explanation. They found a link between growing new vessels and the amount of a growth factor called VEGF (for *v*ascular *e*ndothelial *g*rowth *f*actor). They studied over 500 heart patients. All had a significant block in one or more coronary arteries. Those who made the most VEGF when oxygen supplies were low grew the best network of new blood vessels.

But growing new blood vessels isn't always good. Cancer cells make substances that cause cells in the lining of capillaries to divide and reproduce. Other enzymes break down tissue to make way for the newly forming vessels that feed the tumor. Research on drugs or gene therapy to stop blood flow to a tumor offers promise for the control of cancer in the future.

Is Animal Blood Different from Human Blood?

Blood delivers oxygen to cells in all animals, but—beyond that—the forms and functions of blood vary as greatly as the creatures themselves.

For many animals—including insects, squid, crabs, lobster, crayfish, octopus, horseshoe crab, and earthworms—the oxygen-carrying molecule is not hemoglobin but hemocyanin. It's a much larger molecule than hemoglobin. It contains a copper atom at its center instead of iron. These animals are the real "blue bloods" of the natural world. The copper atom in hemocyanin makes their blood look blue when oxygenated. It's colorless when deoxygenated.

Hemocyanin binds oxygen very efficiently as it encounters the air—either along the walls of an insect's breathing tubes (trachea) or in a spider's hollow, leaflike "book lungs." In earthworms, hemocyanin captures oxygen that diffuses through the skin. A spider's hemocyanin carries oxygen, but it's not packaged in cells. It flows freely, dissolved in the liquid of the spider's blood.

Red blood cells occur in clams, worms, fish, and mammals. Hemoglobin is found both in circulating blood cells and dissolved directly in the blood. Some animals rely on more than one oxygen-carrying molecule. Some have both hemoglobin and hemocyanin. They can change the amount of oxygen delivered to tissues by making more of one or the other.

Animal blood offers us a few surprises. For example:

- In spiders and some other soft-bodied animals that shed their outer hard skeletons, an increase in blood pressure aids in molting. It pushes away old skin and stretches newly exposed legs.

- The octopus may well be the champion of recovery from blood loss. It can move its own volume in fluid from its gut to its blood in five minutes. It can replace a 40 percent blood loss in less than two hours.[10]

- Trout package their hemoglobin in red cells that are larger and less flexible than human red cells. Unlike human red cells, the trout's contain a nucleus.

- Pound for pound, whales and seals have up to 50 percent more blood than humans. Storing oxygen in their blood, not their lungs, sperm whales can stay submerged for up to two hours.

- When a seal begins its underwater dive, the oxygen concentration in its blood is 20 percent. When it surfaces some half-hour later, the concentration has dropped to two percent. Elephant seals have been known to dive nearly a mile deep and stay down for more than an hour.

- Deep-diving birds such as penguins and cormorants have more blood and more blood vessels than other birds. King penguins can dive to almost a third of a mile (500 meters) and stay down for 30 minutes, reports the Museum of Natural History at the University of Georgia. They can do this because of the extra oxygen-carrying capacity of their blood.

- Blue crabs can become anemic. Scientists studied levels of hemocyanin in crabs living in North Carolina's coastal waters. They found low concentrations in some, which may be caused by human-made pollution.

Can Scientists Make Artificial Blood? No, but they are trying. Since the 1950s, researchers have been working to develop "blood substitutes." While no one has been able to duplicate the clotting and disease-fighting functions of real blood, solutions that carry oxygen and carbon dioxide have enjoyed some success.

One promising alternative is a solution of hemoglobin. That sounds simpler than it is. Hemoglobin molecules freed from red cells split into two parts, which the kidneys quickly remove from the blood. Doing so damages the kidneys. Another problem is that free hemoglobin is *too* good at binding oxygen. It won't give it up to the oxygen-hungry cells that need it.

Researchers are trying to engineer hemoglobin molecules to get around these problems. A substance derived from aspirin keeps the two halves of the hemoglobin together, at the same time loosening its structure so it will give up its cargo of oxygen when needed. Surgeons at Duke University have tested a genetically engineered hemoglobin solution in people having hip replacement surgery. "None of the patients experienced any significant side effects or adverse reactions from the product," says Duke anesthesiologist Bruce Leone, "and all of the procedures went without problems."

In 1998, the first such hemoglobin solution was approved by the Food and Drug Administration for use not in humans, but in dogs. The

Biopure Corporation of Cambridge, Massachusetts, began marketing its Oxyglobin® solution to veterinarians. The solution treats anemia in animals. While a blood substitute in the sense that it delivers oxygen to tissues, the product isn't truly artificial. It's made from the blood of cows. It has been tried with human surgical patients in both Europe and the United States with some success.

Still, hemoglobin solutions are a long way from general use in humans. And, even if they do become widely available, their usefulness is limited to a short time period. About half of a hemoglobin solution breaks down in the first twelve hours after transfusion, compared to the 40- to 60-day lifespan of transfused red blood cells.

For this reason, some researchers think a structure more like a red cell might work better. Scientists at McGill University, in Montreal, have tested "packages" of hemoglobin molecules wrapped in a fatty membrane. They have coaxed them to deliver oxygen to cells and to survive for up to 36 hours.

Most of the blood substitutes that have been tried cause blood pressure to rise. Researchers at Rice University have engineered a hemoglobin molecule surrounded by a protective film of large, oily amino acids. In rats, their invention carried oxygen without increasing blood pressure.

If making artificial blood is so difficult, why bother? One reason is the continual shortage of donated blood faced in some areas. Another is concern over infections caught from transfusions (although experts insist the blood supply is safer now than it has ever been). Other advantages include:

- Storage: Room temperature for the artificial stuff; refrigeration for the real thing.

- Shelf life: Synthetic blood can stay fresh for months, even years. Real blood goes bad in six weeks.

- Typing: No matching required for substitutes. Matching for at least eight types (A, B, AB, and O and Rh positive or negative) for real blood.

Incidentally, we may be closer to making artificial blood vessels than to making artificial blood. Scientists at the University of California, San Diego, have made blood vessels from skin and vein cells. Their technique relies on a device called a bioreactor, developed through the U.S. space program. Cells tumble in continuous free fall (a simulation of microgravity) in a solution of oxygen and nutrients. The cells produce collagen and other proteins that form a strong, flexible sheet. When wrapped around a tube and cultured in a nutrient medium, a blood vessel grows. The vessels may someday be used to replace clogged arteries in the heart or legs.

Do Modern Doctors Use Leeches to Bleed Patients?

Yes, and if you are planning a vacation, you may want to visit the world's only leech farm, near Swansea in Wales.

Leeches became part of the doctor's kit as early as 130 B.C. In ancient times, people were bled with leeches to treat everything from obesity to epilepsy—conditions for which the treatment proved totally ineffective. The lack of positive results deterred no one. Into the nineteenth century, bloodletting with leeches "cured" headaches, gout, and many other ailments. In the twentieth century, leeching went out of style until 1985, when doctors at a hospital in Boston reattached the dog-severed ear of a five-year-old boy.

Today, the use of leeches is limited to such cases in which their unique anticlotting properties can prove therapeutic. For example:

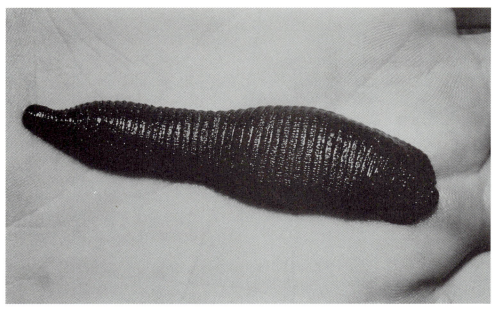

A medicinal leech.

- The leech bites into the skin and releases enzymes that can keep a wound bleeding for hours. While the wound bleeds, veins have time to heal.

- Leeches are especially useful in restoring blood flow to grafted tissue and to fingers, toes, and limbs that have been surgically reattached after an accident.

- The substance from leeches called hirudin has been used experimentally to prevent the clotting of blood that can occur after a heart attack.

Who Ya Gonna Call? Clot Busters!

· · · · ·

The ability or inability of blood to clot is a good example of how, by a finely tuned balancing act, the body has learned how to make use of biological dynamite.

LENNART NILSSON, THE BODY VICTORIOUS

· · · · ·

On the battlefield, a soldier lies dying. He counts his blessings and prepares himself for the end. Blood oozes from a gash in his leg, but— even as he slips into unconsciousness—the wound begins to close. Clots form, and blood flow slows. Miraculously, the soldier lives, though medical care is hours and miles away.

Warm in bed in his Detroit home, a schoolteacher lies dying. Unaware, he plans his lessons for the next day and thinks about a student who needs special help. All day long, his blood has coursed smoothly through his arteries and veins but—

in the moments before sleep comes— a clot no larger than a rice grain forms in his leg and begins the journey to his heart. Although the teacher lives less than a mile from a hospital, he never lives to see that student or teach that lesson.

These stories illustrate the paradox of blood clotting: what saves also kills. A potent force for preserving life can become, in an instant, the silent bullet that destroys it. Since the 1950s, "clot-buster" scientists have been looking for ways to understand the clotting that saves lives and prevent the clotting that ends them.

In general terms, scientists know how clots form. When skin is damaged or a blood vessel torn, platelets make contact with collagen. Collagen is a flexible, elastic material present in both skin and blood vessels. Collagen causes platelets to change. They become spherical and spiny. They stick to the edges of the wound and to each other. They swell and give off a chemical that draws other platelets to the site. The platelets clump and form a plug. If damage is minor, platelets alone can stop the bleeding.

A larger wound is more than platelets can handle alone. Platelets contain granules filled with more than 40 different chemicals. These granules burst and release their contents. Each chemical plays a unique role in the process of clot formation. For example, one causes blood vessels to contract. That decreases blood flow and reduces leakage. Another starts a chain of reactions that turn fibrinogen (already present in the blood) into fibrin. These two equations summarize a process that requires many steps:

- Prothrombin $\xrightarrow{\text{Thrombokinase, Ca++}}$ Thrombin (*Translation*: In the presence of two factors—an enzyme called thrombokinase and charged atoms of calcium—prothrombin changes into thrombin.)
- Fibrinogen $\xrightarrow{\text{Thrombin}}$ Fibrin (*Translation*: In the presence of thrombin, soluble fibrinogen becomes insoluble fibrin.)

The long, sticky fibers of fibrin clump together, creating a web or mesh. The mesh entangles blood cells. It shrinks and squeezes out water. The cells in the web form a clot when fresh, a scab when dry. Both prevent bleeding. An external scab also blocks infectious organisms while new tissue builds. The body handles the "biological dynamite" of the clotting process through this complex series of chemical changes. If any factor or enzyme is missing, a step becomes impossible, and a clot fails to form.

Since the 1950s, researchers have been trying to build a complete and accurate model of every step in the clotting process. They know that at least 14 different substances— perhaps more—are involved. They know that most, if not all, are produced in the liver. All but two are proteins. Six or more depend on

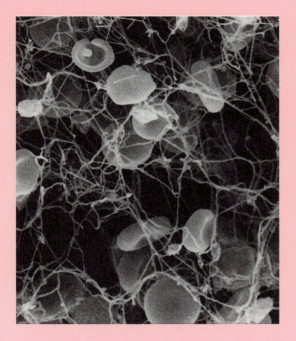

vitamin K to anchor them to cell membranes. Some last for as little as four hours; some last for six days, according to Dade Behring International. But many details remain undiscovered. How are the various clotting factors shaped? How do they attach? How do they perform?

In 1997, three scientists at the University of California at San Diego came up with at least one answer. Glen Spraggon, Stephen Everse, and Russell Doolittle, of the University's Center for Molecular Genetics, created a computer model of fragment D, a part of the fibrinogen molecule. The piece looks a little like a farmer's plow but, "to the trained eye, it's a thing of beauty," says Doolittle.

To gather data for their model, they used a technique called X-ray crystallography. This procedure reveals a swirl or light and dark spots when X rays pass through the molecule. The spots reveal molecular structure to those trained in interpreting them.

But the scientists found that standard laboratory X rays couldn't give them all the information they needed. They used a synchrotron in England to get X rays of a different wavelength. The resulting picture revealed how one part of a fibrinogen molecule is shaped. That knowledge, in turn, increases hopes of finding ways to induce clotting when it could save a life and block it when it could kill.

In other laboratories, clot-busting scientists are looking for new and better ways to treat or prevent the clotting associated with heart disease, stroke, and some inherited blood diseases. For example:

- Warren Lockett, at Wayne State University in Detroit, has worked with drugs that lower blood pressure by helping the body eliminate excess fluid. One such drug seems to block blood clotting by preventing platelets from clumping.

- Johns Hopkins University scientists are investigating one of the molecules in the clotting sequence that makes platelets sticky. If a way could be found to block it, clotting might be prevented.

- At the University of Delaware, researcher Mary Ann McLane studies proteins in snake venom that stop fibrinogen from binding to platelets. McLane hopes to develop the proteins into a treatment for blood clots that form in arteries.

- Stanford University researchers have moved a step closer to creating "self-cleaning" blood vessels. They have transplanted into arteries a gene that turns them into tPA super factories. (The abbreviation tPA stands for *t*issue *p*lasminogen *a*ctivator, a protein that breaks clots apart.)

And, proving that there's more than one way to skin a clot, University of Pennsylvania physicians have implanted filters in the large veins of accident victims. People recovering from fractures may rest in bed for days or weeks. Inactivity raises their risk of developing a clot. But if implanted early in treatment, the filter acts like a miniature catcher's mitt. It snares a clot before it can become life-threatening. The filter can't prevent every incident, but along with genes and drugs, it's yet another weapon in the arsenal of those savvy scientists, the "clot busters."

CHAPTER FOUR

ABOUT WHEN THINGS GO WRONG

The heart in thee is the heart of all; not a valve, not a wall, not an intersection is there anywhere in nature, but one blood rolls uninterruptedly an endless circulation through all.

• RALPH WALDO EMERSON •

What's Heart Disease?

The terms "heart disease" and "cardiovascular disease" include several different disorders. One is ischemia, or reduced circulation to a part of the body. The symptoms depend on the organs involved. A blocked artery in the leg, for example, brings on pain during exercise that disappears afterward. Ischemia in a kidney raises blood pressure. Silent ischemia is so named because blood supply to the heart is restricted, but the person has no symptoms and feels no pain.

Congestive heart failure describes a heart unable to pump enough blood to meet the body's needs. Ischemia to the heart muscle can bring on heart failure, but it's not the only cause. High blood pressure can do it, too. The American Heart Association estimates that three to four million Americans have ischemia in the heart without even knowing it.

As we grow older, our vessels thicken and stiffen. That's called *arterio*sclerosis, and it comes to affect most people later in life. More serious is the damage to arteries called *athero*sclerosis. Injury to an artery's slippery lining causes plaque to accumulate at the site. Plaque deposits are masses of dead cells, blood-clotting factors, fat, calcium, cholesterol, and other substances. They slow or block blood flow. Continuous healing and scarring around the plaque causes the artery to narrow even more. The vessel hardens. Blood flow decreases further. Cells served by the vessel starve for oxygen.

Atherosclerosis in the arteries and capillaries of the heart's own blood supply is the most common cause of what we call heart disease. In this case, the cells that starve and die are those of the heart muscle itself.

What's Angina? Nerve cells in the heart fire in response to the low levels of oxygen that come with ischemia (insufficient blood supply). They send pain signals to the brain. Because of the interconnection of nerves in the upper body, the brain may misinterpret where the signal is coming from. The pain called angina may be felt in the chest, arm, neck, jaw, shoulder, or back. Exercise, anxiety, excitement, or cold weather can provoke angina. Sometimes it comes on for no reason at all. In a sense, angina may be the heart patient's best friend. It sends most people off to a doctor before obstruction of the blood supply to the heart gets worse.

How Big a Problem Is Heart Disease?

At age 40, the lifetime risk of developing some form of cardiovascular disease is one in two for healthy men. It's one in three for healthy women. That means that half of all forty-year-old men will develop cardiovascular disease before they die. So will a third of all women.[1] Cardiovascular diseases take a life every 33 seconds, according to the American Heart Association. These diseases are the number one killer of both men and women in the United States.

Is Heart Disease Inherited?

To answer that question, think probabilities. Few things are certain, but some are more predictable than others. For example, flip a coin and the chance of heads or tails is the same: 50:50, or one-half. Only two outcomes are possible. They occur with equal frequency. With inherited disorders such as sickle-cell disease (see page 68), the outcome is predictable. That's because we know that one pair of genes causes the disease. For two parents who each carry the gene, the chance of having a child with sickle-cell disease is one in four with each pregnancy.

Other cardiovascular diseases run in families, but many genes play a part. Also, environmental factors such as diet, exercise, and smoking make a big difference. So, prediction must consider many variables. Family history is one of them. In many cases, it increases risk. For example, a person whose mother or father had a sudden heart stoppage is 50 percent more likely to have one as well. The risk rises to 70 percent if the affected relative was a brother or sister.[2]

Some other factors that increase the risk of heart disease also run in families. A family history of high blood pressure, diabetes, or high cholesterol makes heart disease more likely, but don't expect certainties. Statistics predict for populations, not individuals. That's why many people are the only one in their family to have heart disease. It's also why some people escape heart disease despite many cases among close relatives.

How Are Cardiovascular Diseases Treated?

Treatment depends on the condition and its severity. Diet, exercise, and stopping smoking are recommended for nearly everyone. Drugs to lower cholesterol, decrease blood pressure, or speed or slow heart rate are prescribed when needed. Daily small doses of aspirin can prevent blood clotting in patients at risk.

For those facing higher risks, a procedure called angioplasty opens blocked arteries in the heart. The heart doctor inserts a catheter, or tube, into the blocked artery. Another catheter equipped with a tiny uninflated balloon passes through the guiding tube. When the balloon is inflated, it pushes against the block. The pressure forces plaque back into the artery wall.

Once pushed open, the artery lets blood flow more freely. After the tubes are removed, a flexible metal coil, called a "stent" is often put in place. The stent prevents the block from returning. So does a low dose of beta radiation given after the angioplasty. About half a million angioplasties are performed in the United States every year.[3] The success rate exceeds 90 percent.

If atherosclerosis blocks the largest arteries of the heart, or if tests show that the left ventricle is not working properly, the doctor may

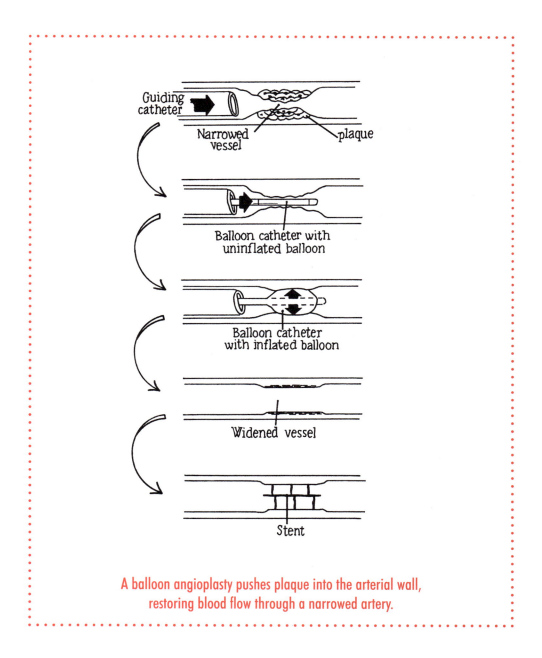

Guiding catheter

Narrowed vessel

plaque

Balloon catheter with uninflated balloon

Balloon catheter with inflated balloon

Widened vessel

Stent

A balloon angioplasty pushes plaque into the arterial wall, restoring blood flow through a narrowed artery.

recommend coronary bypass surgery. Just as engineers build a detour around a collapsed tunnel, surgeons insert new vessels to route blood around a blockage. About 600,000 bypass operations are performed annually in the United States, nearly half of them on people younger than 65.[4]

The usual method of bypass surgery requires dividing the breastbone and separating the ribs. Someday, robots may spare bypass patients pain, recovery time, and scars. New surgical systems allow pencil-sized robotic arms to be inserted into the chest. Video cameras provide three-dimensional, enlarged views. The surgeon moves the robot's arms from a remote control panel.

About 10 to 15 percent of heart disease patients cannot have angioplasty or bypass surgery, according to Cedars–Sinai Medical Center. For them, a new technique called TMR (for *trans*m*yocardial laser *r*evascularization) offers promise. To perform the procedure, doctors insert a laser into a small incision in the chest. They guide the laser light to cut tiny channels into the muscle. In response, the heart grows new blood vessels.

Someday, even TMR may be out of date. In 1999, doctors at Toronto General Hospital took healthy heart cells from pigs that had suffered heart attacks. After growing the cells in the laboratory, they injected some into the damaged areas of the pigs' hearts. A month later, the damaged regions had thickened. Motion improved, as did pumping action. The pigs that received the injections were more active and gained more weight than those that didn't.

In 1998, German scientists used a protein called FGF-1 (the GF means growth *f*actor) to stimulate blood vessels to grow in the heart muscle. In 20 human volunteers, the new vessels doubled or even tripled blood flow.[5] Researchers in Boston have tried a different approach. They inject a gene that directs cells to make a growth factor called VEGF. They want to find out if the gene will direct heart cells to make growth factor and build new blood vessels as a result.

What's a Heart Attack?

When an artery wall is damaged, the body's repair mechanism responds. It causes blood to clot at the site. While a clot helps heal a skin wound, it causes trouble in a blood vessel. It's called a thrombus if it stays where it forms. It's an embolism if it breaks loose and travels to another site. In either case, the results can be sudden and severe. A clot that forms or lodges in the heart blocks blood flow to a part of the heart muscle. Cells die, and heart function falters or ceases. That's a heart attack.

Some heart attacks occur without warning. Others give signs such as:

- Pressure, fullness, squeezing, or aching pain in the center of the chest

- Pain in shoulders, neck, arms, jaw, upper abdomen, or back

- Lightheadedness, fainting, nausea, shortness of breath

- Anxiety, nervousness, or cold and sweaty skin

- Paleness

- Increased or irregular heart rate

- Feeling of impending doom

A heart attack that stops the heart is called "sudden cardiac death." Heart stoppage kills 250,000 Americans every year, according to the American Heart Association. Rupturing or eroding plaque (fatty deposits) causes the heart to cease beating. A plaque deposit provokes a clot large enough to block a major artery in the heart.

- Sudden weakness or numbness in the face, arm, leg, or on one side of the body

- Sudden dimness, blurring or loss of vision, especially in one eye

- Sudden loss of speech or trouble talking or understanding speech

- Sudden, severe headache

- A sudden fall or unexplained dizziness or unsteadiness

Are Any Heart Diseases Contagious?

Yes. The common bacteria that cause strep throat can settle in the heart, infecting its inner lining or valves. This is rheumatic fever, which—while rare in the United States—is a common cause of heart-valve diseases in third-world countries. Infections coming from other areas of the body can also settle in the heart valves. This is called bacterial endocarditis. Often, antibiotics can stop such infections if treatment is started early. If it's not, the bacteria can destroy heart tissue.

Some infections produce symptoms so similar to those of blocked arteries in the heart that only an expert can tell the difference. *Trypanosoma cruzi* is a single-cell protozoan. It burrows into the heart muscle and causes Chagas' disease. The disease is a major killer of young and middle-aged people in Central and South America. Sometimes, it shows up in people who immigrate to the United States from Mexico and points south. The organism lives in farm animals. The bite of a common insect transfers it to humans, where it reproduces in the brain, nerves, skeletal muscle, and heart.

Do Chest Pains Always Signal a Heart Attack?

No. On the average, only a third of those who experience chest pains actually have angina[7]. Other causes of chest pain include indigestion, injury, inflammation in the cartilage or muscles of the ribs, spasms in a coronary artery, or panic attacks. Teenagers sometimes experience chest pains, but 90 percent of the time, the pain is caused by normal growth in their bones and muscles. Despite the odds, never ignore chest pains, and never let your loved ones ignore them either. Only a physician can diagnose the cause.

Is Fainting a Sign of a Heart or Blood Problem?

For most young people, fainting isn't serious. It happens when blood pressure drops and heart rate slows, resulting in too little oxygen reaching the brain. Short on oxygen, brain cells slow their release of energy from nutrients. Consciousness lapses. Eating too little food or drinking too little water is sometimes to blame. Or blood pools in the legs while a person stands still for long periods (as you might, for example, while singing in a choir.) Stress is another common cause. Warning signals may include nausea, lightheadedness, or sweaty, clammy skin. A gradual blackening of vision or ringing in the ears may precede fainting. After a minute or two of lying down (albeit involuntarily!), blood flow to the brain resumes, and consciousness returns.

Fainting without warning or during exercise sometimes signals a more serious problem. So do other symptoms, such as a pounding or very rapid heartbeat, dizziness, weakness, shortness of breath, or chest pain. Although rarer in teens than in older people, heart failure, blocks in coronary arteries, and defective valves can cause sudden death. If you faint, don't take a chance. See your doctor.

Is the Number of Heart Attacks and Strokes Decreasing?

No, it's increasing, despite strides made in prevention and treatment. The reason involves an irony of modern life. We die of heart disease and strokes because—on the average—we are living longer than any generation before us. The U.S. population in the year 2000 had almost twice as many senior citizens as it did in 1940. The longer the life, the greater the risk.

The picture is brighter, however, when viewed from a different angle. Treatment of high blood pressure decreases the chance of stroke by 60 to 80 percent. In addition, modern treatments for heart attacks have reduced the risk of death from 40 percent to less than 10 percent.[8]

What's an Aneurysm?

An aneurysm is a weak spot in a blood vessel. The spot can expand like a balloon and burst, causing stroke or death. Aneurysms often occur in the aorta, the large artery that carries blood from the heart to the body. The rupture of an aneurysm in the aorta can cause massive internal bleeding and rapid death. The pressure of blood collecting from a burst aneurysm in the brain can impair movement, speech, or some other brain function.

Aren't Women Safe from Heart Disease?

While it's true that men—on the average—have more heart attacks at an earlier age, women aren't immune. "Cardiovascular disease kills more than half a million women each year. That's more than the next 14 causes of death combined," says former American Heart Association President Lynn Smaha. Also, many women don't realize that stroke is as big a risk for them as it is for men. Stroke is the leading cause of major disability for both sexes, and the third leading cause of death, according to the American Heart Association.

Women are less likely to have a heart attack or a stroke before menopause than after. For that reason, physicians and scientists have suspected that taking hormones after menopause could reduce the risk of cardiovascular disease. Indeed, many studies have confirmed that hypothesis, but others have not. It's possible that female hormones lower levels of clotting factors and cholesterol in the blood. They may also make blood less sticky or viscous, but it may be a number of years before anyone knows for sure.

Aren't Young People Safe from Heart Disease?

Half of all heart attacks strike people younger than 65.[9] While heart disease and heart attacks are rare in children and teens, doctors think that the process of plaque formation begins in youth. Therefore, they advise regular exercise, a low-fat diet, and medical checkups for children and young adults alike.

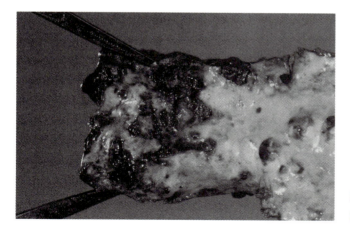

A plaque deposit taken from an artery

What Drugs Do Doctors Use to Treat Heart Disease?

Drugs are powerful weapons in the cardiologist's arsenal, and many heart patients take medication daily. One of the oldest heart drugs—in continuous use for over 200 years—is digitalis. It works by inducing sodium channels to let calcium into heart muscle cells. The change in charge causes the heart to beat with greater strength. Another time-honored treatment, nitroglycerin, is the same compound used in making dynamite. It widens narrowed vessels and makes blood flow more freely.

A number of different drugs reduce blood pressure. For example:

- Diuretics increase excretion of sodium and water from the kidneys. With less water, blood volume is reduced, and blood pressure along with it.

- People with angina sometimes take beta-blockers. These drugs stop stimuli to the heart that can make it beat too rapidly. They also reduce the strength of the heart's contraction, which lowers blood pressure.

- Channel blockers stop calcium from entering blood vessel walls. That relaxes and dilates the arteries.

- After a heart attack, some people take ACE (for *a*ngiotensin-*c*onverting *e*nzyme) inhibitors. They block production of an enzyme involved in making a hormone that causes blood vessels to tighten. This relaxes and opens blood vessels, lowers blood pressure, and reduces the heart's workload.

Some drugs dissolve blood clots. Others, called anticoagulants or "blood thinners," prevent them. The most commonly prescribed anticoagulant is aspirin. It makes platelets less sticky, so blood is less likely to clot. A baby-sized aspirin tablet taken daily can reduce heart attack risk by 25

Digitalis comes from the foxglove plant, and was harvested by hand for years until chemists came up with a synthetic version.

to 50 percent.[10] It also lowers the chances of first and second strokes. The American Heart Association says simply taking an aspirin when the symptoms of heart attack appear could save 10,000 lives a year.[11] Drugs that lower blood cholesterol levels have become widely used in recent years. They either decrease absorption of cholesterol from food or interfere with the liver's production of it. Also, women past menopause can choose to take estrogen, a female hormone. Estrogen seems to have a number of benefits, including reducing cholesterol levels and relaxing blood vessels—although whether estrogen prevents heart attacks is open to question.

What Is Leukemia, and How Is It Treated?

All cancers are abnormal cells produced in excessive numbers. Several different kinds of cancer strike bone marrow, blood, and the lymphatic system. For example:

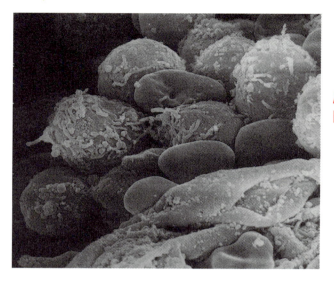

A magnification of hairy cell leukemia

- Lymphoma: Abnormal lymphocytes—a type of leukocyte— increase in number. They crowd out healthy cells and grow tumors in lymph nodes. (Hodgkin's disease is one kind of lymphoma.)

- Myeloma: Plasma cells—another type of leukocyte—multiply out of control, destroying bone marrow and interfering with the manufacture of all kinds of blood cells. They also interfere with the production of antibodies, making the person prone to infections.

- Leukemia: Immature, inactive leukocytes accumulate in the blood and bone marrow. They hinder the production of all other cells, including red cells, white cells, and platelets. With too few red cells, the patient's tissues starve for oxygen. A shortage of normal leukocytes invites infections. Too few platelets lead to bruising and bleeding.

Anyone can get any of these blood or lymph cancers. The causes are largely unknown, although chemicals or radiation are suspected in some cases. Four major types of leukemia have been identified, depending on what cells are involved and how quickly the disease progresses. In one type, the bone marrow produces 50 to 60 times the normal number of white blood cells, and many of them are abnormal.[12] Too few red cells circulate, and those that do can't do their job properly. White cells clog capillaries and interfere with the work of internal organs.

Doctors treat leukemia with strong drugs that kill leukemic cells. Radiation is also used. It damages abnormal cells and prevents them from multiplying. Bone-marrow transplants are often employed as well. Two types are common. One uses the patient's own healthy marrow cells, cleared of cancer cells and returned to the bone. The second kind involves a blood marrow donor—sometimes a relative, sometimes not. Donations that are carefully "tissue typed"—matching the proteins of the donor closely with those of the recipient—can be as successful as donations from a brother or sister.

Becoming more widely used are transplants of stem cells from umbilical cords. Stem cells develop into other kinds of blood cells. They can, in many cases, successfully substitute for bone marrow. "The advantage of cord blood cells . . . is that they are still immunologcially naive. They have not learned to identify with a particular host [body] and, therefore, are more adaptable than mature marrow cells to new environments," says Patrick Stiff, director of the bone marrow transplant program at Loyola University Medical Center, in Chicago, Illinois.

Each year, treatment of blood cancers improves. For example, in 1960, the five-year survival rate of children with one form of leukemia was only four percent. By the mid-1990s, it had risen to 80 percent, according to the Leukemia Society of America.

How Does Cancer Spread Through the Bloodstream?

In 1889, the English surgeon Stephen Paget published his "seed-and-soil hypothesis" to explain the spread of cancer from one organ to another. The seeds of a plant, Paget wrote, "are carried in all directions; but they can only live and grow if they fall on congenial soil."[13] He believed that cancer cells traveled in every direction but thrived only where they found the right environment. His idea might explain why prostate cancers so often spread to the bone and colon tumors spread to the liver.

In 1928, the American James Ewing offered a different idea: the "mechanical hypothesis." He thought that patterns of blood flow might explain spread. The first organ encountered in the bloodstream would most likely be the first organ infected. For example, the lung is often the first organ most tumor cells encounter. That fits with the fact that the lungs frequently develop cancers that start in other places.

As so often happens in science, both Paget and Ewing turned out to be right. In many cases, spread can be predicted from patterns of blood flow. But a tumor will not grow unless it finds the right conditions. What are the right conditions? The presence of molecules that let cancer cells move into an organ and multiply there.

The cancer cells, Paget's "seeds," must also possess certain characteristics. Ironically, some of the same molecules that protect the body against infection also make it vulnerable to the spread of cancer. "Inflammatory cells—neutrophils, monocytes, lymphocytes—are designed to be able to go across blood vessels very well," says Bruce Zetter, of the Harvard Medical School. "And that's also the hallmark of the metastatic [spreading] cell. It has to be able to zip in and out of blood vessels and migrate across tissues."[14]

What Are Varicose Veins, and How Are They Treated?

The word "varicose" means twisted and stretched. It describes well the knotty, bluish clusters of distended veins that can appear— usually in the legs, and usually in older people. They occur because valves in the veins fail to close properly, allowing backflow. The extra weight of blood presses on the vein and stretches it. That creates even more pressure on other valves, causing them to fail too. Eventually, veins protrude and swell near enough to the skin to be

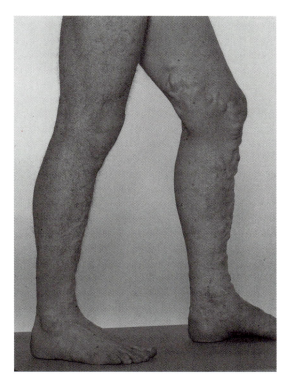

A patient with varicose veins

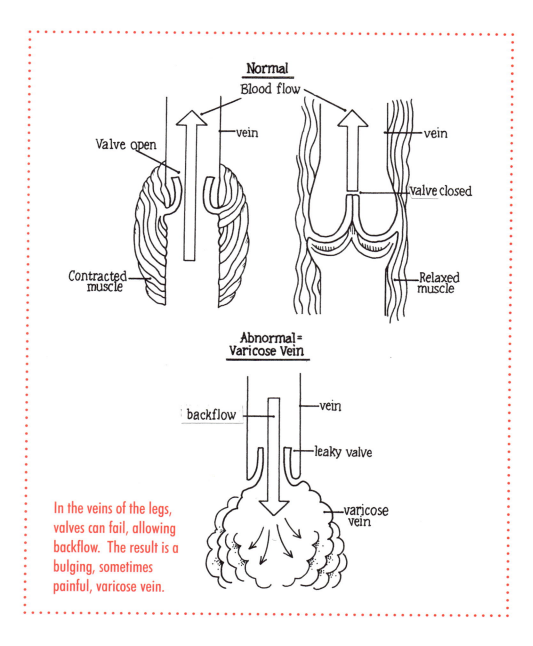

Normal

Blood flow

Valve open

vein

vein

Valve closed

Contracted muscle

Relaxed muscle

Abnormal= Varicose Vein

backflow

vein

leaky valve

varicose vein

In the veins of the legs, valves can fail, allowing backflow. The result is a bulging, sometimes painful, varicose vein.

visible. Varicose veins should not be confused with "spider veins," which are tiny, weblike clusters of blue or red veins lying just under the skin.

In some people, varicose veins cause no symptoms. Others experience far worse aching, pain, swelling, and sores that won't heal. The tendency toward varicose veins is inherited. Some people are born with too few valves or valves that weaken over time. Inactivity can make matters worse, as can pregnancy, long hours of standing, or being overweight. About one in ten men and one in four women in the United States have varicose veins.[15] Women face a higher risk, because female hormones relax the walls of veins and allow them to stretch.

Treatment includes elevating the legs above the heart to facilitate blood flow to the legs. Elastic support stockings assist muscle action. In severe cases, doctors inject chemicals to shrink damaged veins and re-route circulation into healthier ones. In even worse cases, surgeons remove distended veins entirely.

What's Hypertension, and How Is It Treated?

Hypertension isn't a nervous condition. It's blood pressure that runs consistently too high. Moving too hard and too fast, the stream of blood damages the fragile inner linings of arteries. It can also injure the kidneys, brain, heart, and other organs. Hypertension is sometimes called a "silent killer," because it has no symptoms. One-third of the 50 million Americans who have it don't know.[16] A blood-pressure check done by a health-care professional is the only way to find out.

Research has uncovered differences among people that help explain why some have high blood pressure and others don't. A number of steps may be involved. Here's an example:

1. The kidneys of some individuals make too much of an enzyme called renin.

2. Renin, in turn, triggers the production of hormones that constrict arteries.

3. Those hormones cause the release of yet another hormone. It causes the kidneys to retain sodium (salt) and excrete potassium.

4. Increased salt levels, in turn, keep more water in the body (water retention).

5. Water retention increases blood volume.

6. The heart must work harder to push more blood through narrower vessels. Just as water pumped forcefully into a small pipe creates a lot of pressure, so does blood. Its pressure rises.

In 1998, the Americans Robert Furchgott, Louis Ignarro, and Ferid Murad shared the Nobel Prize in Medicine. They discovered another factor that affects blood pressure. The colorless gas nitric oxide acts as a signaling molecule in the blood. It relaxes blood vessels and dilates them. A lack of nitric oxide in the blood—or a failure of the vessels to respond to it—can narrow vessels and raise pressure.

We can't do anything about the renin or nitric oxide in our blood, but we can make choices about what we eat. Doctors usually recommend weight loss to lower blood pressure. Researchers in Dayton, Ohio, studied healthy people ages 18 to 71 for an average of 13 years. "People getting fatter at a higher rate were the ones who tended to have their blood pressure increasing at a higher rate," says Roger Siervogel, a professor at Wright State University. "Those with lower levels of changes in body fat tended to have smaller increases, and in some cases, decreases in blood pressure," he says.

Exercise is also important in keeping blood pressure down. Researchers at the University of Maryland, in College Park, found that blood pressure goes down and stays down for up to 15 hours after 45 minutes of exercise.[17] Other ways to lower blood pressure include eating less salt, avoiding alcohol, and taking medicines doctors prescribe for that purpose. Stress reduction can help, too. Researchers in Israel taught heart patients how to handle their hostile feelings. Their subjects lowered their diastolic blood pressure an average of ten percent.[18]

And, if all that's not enough, consider getting a pet. Researchers at the University of Buffalo studied a group of hypertensive New York stockbrokers. Their subjects were given prescription medicines and social support—the human variety. In addition, half were asked to take in a cat or a dog as part of their treatment regimen. After six months, subjects were tested for their responses to stress. Pet owners experienced half the rise in blood pressure of their petless peers.

Does Too Much Salt Cause High Blood Pressure?

Yes, but only in certain people. It's a matter of genetic makeup, and several genes may be involved.

One gene that researchers know causes "salt-sensitivity" is the ACE gene (short for *angiotensin converting enzyme*). Angiotensin makes blood vessels contract. That raises blood pressure. The ACE gene controls how much angiotensin is released into the body. If the ACE gene is flawed, it can cause too much angiotensin to flow into the bloodstream, raising blood pressure too much. If that variant of the gene is present, as little as half a teaspoon of extra salt can raise blood pressure by five points, according to the American Heart Association. Drugs called ACE inhibitors break this chain of events and relieve high blood pressure in many people—whether they are salt-sensitive or not.

What Causes a Heart to Enlarge? High blood pressure, a heart attack, or a disorder of an endocrine gland can cause the heart to grow bigger. "What the heart does is try to compensate for that damage by increasing its size to achieve greater cardiac output," says Eric Olson, of the University of Texas Southwestern Medical Center. But an enlarged heart is an inefficient pump, and too often heart failure results. Olson and his research team experimented with mice. They found that enlargement results from a protein called calcineurin. When calcium levels rise, calcineurin activates another protein that enters the nucleus of heart muscle cells. It causes the cells to grow. Olson is experimenting with drugs that block calcineurin in hopes of preventing heart enlargement.

What Should I Do if I Think Someone May Be Having a Heart Attack? First, don't waste valuable time wondering if you might be wrong. Better to err on the side of caution than risk losing a life. Then, follow these steps recommended by the American Heart Association:

1. After listening for breathing and checking for a pulse, **call 911** (or the emergency medical services number for your community). Be ready to describe the symptoms you observe: chest pain, breathing difficulties, fainting.

2. **If there is no pulse or breathing, begin cardiopulmonary resuscitation (CPR).** The technique keeps blood moving and oxygen flowing to the brain. It buys valuable time until full breathing and blood-pumping functions can be restored. If you don't know what to do, ask the dispatcher to direct you until help arrives.

3. **Give aspirin.** If the person can breathe and communicate, give him or her one or two aspirins to chew, or dissolve the tablets in water. They'll be absorbed more quickly than tablets swallowed whole. Aspirin may dissolve small clots blocking the coronary arteries and make the heart attack less severe. Studies have shown that aspirin taken within the first few minutes of a heart attack can save one life in four.[19]

What Is CPR, and How Does It Work?

CPR stands for cardiopulmonary resuscitation. It is a combination of mouth-to-mouth breathing, which supplies oxygen to the lungs, and pressure on the chest to circulate blood. CPR can keep breathing going and the heart pumping until emergency medical services arrive.

If you take a class in CPR (and you should!), you'll learn first how to tilt the victim's head back and clear the airway into the lungs. Next, you'll learn to breathe into the victim's mouth to inflate the lungs. Starting a stopped heart requires compression. Pushing against the breastbone in a regular counting rhythm does that. The steps in CPR are precise and exacting. You really can't learn them by reading, but you can learn them in classes sponsored by the American Heart Association, the Red Cross, or the emergency response units in many communities.

What Does a Defibrillator Do?

To understand what this device does, you must first understand fibrillation itself. Sometimes, without warning, heart cells become deprived of oxygen and become very acidic. Under acid conditions, the ion pumps and channels that usually maintain charges inside and outside the cells fail. Too many positively charged ions rush in too quickly. If this change in chemistry doesn't kill the cells, it can make them contract at breakneck speed. Lacking coordinated action, the heart fails to pump blood. "If you held the fibrillating heart in your hand," says Arun Holden, of the University of Leeds in England, "it would feel like a ball of writhing worms, quivering chaotically."[20]

With no blood being pushed from the heart, blood pressure drops to zero. Without oxygen, the brain can't work. Unconsciousness is immediate. Death of brain cells begins in three minutes. Six minutes without oxygen, and the brain suffers permanent, irreversible damage. Fibrillation must be stopped, and it must be stopped quickly.

A defibrillator sends an electric shock through the heart. The shock resets the charges across cell membranes. In conjunction with CPR, defibrillation stops the quivering and returns the beat to its normal, coordinated pace.

A Day in the Life of a Perfusionist

• • • • •

I would advise anyone who is seriously considering perfusion as a career to spend as much time as possible in an operating room. Make sure this environment is right for you.

DEBRA SUE DOUGLASS

• • • • •

Debra Sue Douglass gets up at five in the morning, when most people are still snug in bed. She works as chief perfusionist at a large teaching hospital in Texas. She must get to work by six to "prepare her circuit" before the first patient enters the operating room.

What's a perfusionist? What's preparing a circuit? Debby explains: "A perfusionist operates a heart/lung machine. Preparing a circuit means assembling the machine so it's ready for surgery."

Heart/lung machines are not new. In 1953, the Philadelphia physician John Gibbon used one he had invented. It allowed him to perform the first successful open-heart surgery on an adult. Much better machines have been developed since then, but all do the same job. They take over the patient's circulation and gas exchange. That lets the surgeon work on a heart that is not moving. In open-heart surgery, doctors replace damaged or diseased valves, repair dead heart muscle, insert bypass vessels around blocked ones, or transplant entire hearts.

Before dawn, Debby studies her patients' records. If the first opera-

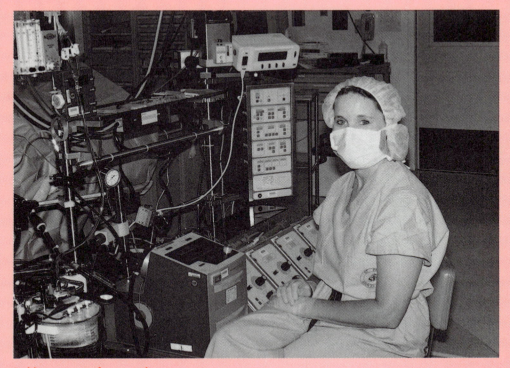

Debby prepares for open-heart surgery.

tion is coronary bypass surgery (page 92), she waits while the surgeon "harvests" a vein from the leg and an artery from the chest. Both will be used as replacement vessels to carry blood around blocked arteries of the heart. Not until the surgeon prepares for work on the heart itself does Debby begin substituting the mechanical pump for the living one.

Those first minutes of transferring circulation and gas exchange to the heart/lung machine are stressful. "I do about five things at the same time while monitoring another ten," Debby says. After that, she must maintain the patient's blood pressure, blood flow through the body, temperature, oxygen and carbon dioxide levels, and electrolytes. She makes sure no damage occurs in the heart muscle. "I'm the life support for the patient," she says. When surgery ends, she weans her patient off the machine before sending him or her to intensive care for recovery.

Debby became a certified perfusionist in 1983. She's a graduate of the Texas Heart Institute School of Perfusion Technology in Houston. She studied there after receiving a bachelor's degree in zoology from Arizona State University. "My career in perfusion was truly by accident," she says. "All my life I planned to become a veterinarian. Then about halfway through my senior year in college, I realized I didn't want to be a vet. In six months' time I would be graduating, and I didn't have a clue as to what I was going to do with the rest of my life."

Debby asked advice from her best friend, whose father was a cardiovascular surgeon. The physician suggested to Debby that perfusion might be the right career for her. Debby believes that when one door closes, another opens. Perfusion was

During open-heart surgery, the heart stops. The heart/lung machine takes over both gas exchange and blood pumping.

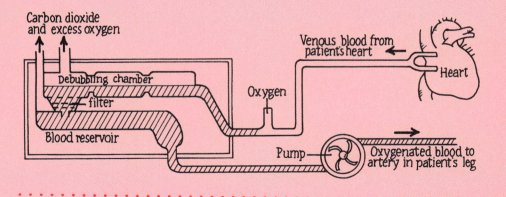

the door she stepped through, and she has never regretted her decision.

As chief perfusionist, Debby has duties extending beyond operating the heart/lung machine. She supervises four other members of the perfusion team, schedules perfusionists for six hospitals, orders supplies and equipment, and works with heart surgeons on research and education. "This job requires a person to handle stress and emergency situations with a cool head and a calm hand. A perfusionist must be able to improvise in an instant and anticipate the unthinkable. Long hours and little sleep can be expected, but helping people is the reward," she says.

Debby has seen tremendous changes in her profession in a short time. When she was an infant in 1958, heart surgery was in its infancy too. "At that time, pioneering surgeons were just beginning to take their thoughts and ideas to the research lab," she says. Another two decades would pass before open-heart surgery was routinely done in major cities. Another ten would go by before bypass surgery became almost as common as an appendectomy.

In her off-duty hours, Debby enjoys her Texas home, friends, family, and two cats. She skis, cycles, camps, cooks, gardens, and fishes. "I play a mean game of pinochle, and I own more power tools than anybody on my block," she says. "Most evenings you'll find me at the Jazzercise center or walking with my neighbors," she adds with a grin.

On the go again before dawn the next day, Debby never tires of her career. "To know that you have done your best to help people improve their quality of life is very gratifying," she says. The value of her work came home to her when a neighbor's father-in-law suffered from deterioration of the heart muscle. He longed to play with his grandchildren but didn't have the strength. A heart transplant gave him a new lease on life.

"I met this man several months later," Debby says, "and found out I had been the perfusionist during his surgery. I saw him play with his granddaughters. I saw the smile that beamed across his face. That was one of my greatest rewards."

• • • • •

CHAPTER FIVE

23 QUESTIONS

ABOUT YOUR HEALTHY HEART

Here is bread, which strengthens [the] heart,
and therefore called the staff of life.

• Matthew Henry •

Is a Heart Attack Preventable?

Yes, in many cases; but to answer that question fully, you must consider risk factors.

Nothing in life is risk free. When you step into a crosswalk, you take a chance that a careless driver will hit you. The risk of an accident increases if traffic is heavy, the streets are icy, or the signal light is broken. Those risks lie outside your control, but that doesn't mean you are helpless. You can cross at the corner, look both ways, and walk carefully. If you cross against the light, weave through moving traffic, or stand in the middle of the road, you make an accident more likely. None of these behaviors guarantees that you will be hit, but you tilt the odds against yourself with such choices.

Risk factors for heart disease work the same way. Some you can control, and some you cannot. Gender is a risk factor. Before age 65, males have a greater risk of heart disease than females. After that, risks are equal,[1] and risks increase with age, regardless of sex. Ancestry is another risk factor. African-Americans face a greater risk than Caucasians. Diabetes or a family history of heart disease raises the odds. People who lack supportive emotional ties to family and friends and those who have incomes near the poverty level also face higher risks. Even the weather may be a risk factor. French researchers reported that an 18-degree (F.) decrease in temperature on a single day raised the chance of a first heart attack by 13 percent.[2]

You can't change the weather, and you certainly can't change your sex, ethnic group, family history, or age. You may not be able to improve your social relationships or your family's income easily either. But factors that are impossible or difficult to change neither doom you to heart disease nor let you off the hook. Experts at the University of Michigan Preventive Cardiology Services estimate that lifestyle changes can prevent more than half of all heart-related deaths.

Opportunities to prevent heart disease occur in noting those risk factors that you *can* do something about. They include high blood cholesterol, high blood pressure, physical inactivity, obesity, stress, and, *most of all*, smoking.

Although it takes a doctor to diagnose high cholesterol and high blood pressure, it doesn't always take a doctor to correct them. A healthy diet and regular exercise can often do the trick. And, since risk factors interact, reducing one risk may well reduce another. For example, the risks of physical inactivity and obesity often occur together. Many people find that getting more exercise helps them lose weight even without a change in eating habits. Weight loss, in turn, improves both cholesterol and blood-pressure measurements.

Reducing stress through enjoyable activities can yield physical health benefits, too, especially if a more relaxed attitude steers you past the refrigerator or the cigarette counter. A positive attitude can help after a heart attack as well as before. Psychologist Vicki Helgeson, at Carnegie Mellon University, found that heart-attack patients who scored high on measures of self-esteem, optimism, and control over their lives were less likely to have another heart attack than others who scored low. Also, laboratory research shows that social ties and support reduce the threat of heart disease. "People need to realize that they do need each other to stay healthy," says Redford Williams, of Duke University.

The single best thing you can do for your heart is never to start smoking or—if you start—to quit immediately. Why? See the next two questions for only a few of the many reasons.

How Does Smoking Cause Heart Disease?

Smoking reduces the supply of oxygen to the heart and other muscles. It elevates cholesterol levels. It increases the risk of blood clots and induces irregular heart rhythms and speeds. Carbon monoxide in smoke binds with red cells and keeps them from delivering oxygen properly. Nicotine stimulates the heart to beat faster. Smoking raises blood pressure and damages artery linings, making the buildup of plaque more likely. Clotting becomes more likely too, because smoking changes the size and structure of platelets. Smoking reduces HDLs and raises LDLs.

Smoking increases the body's production of an immune substance called C-reactive protein. Clot-busting drugs used to treat heart attacks don't work as well in people who have high levels of that protein. Boston researchers found that women with the highest levels of C-reactive protein are five times more likely to suffer heart attacks and seven times more likely to have a stroke than women with low levels.[3] Similar findings applied to men.

A person needn't be a heavy smoker to suffer from smoking's hazards. The American Heart Association reports on a study of 13,000 men in the United States, Europe, and Japan followed over 25 years. Those who smoked between one and nine cigarettes a day had a 30 percent higher risk of death from heart disease or lung cancer than those of the same age who did not smoke at all. For men who smoked ten or more cigarettes a day, the risk soared to 80 percent, according to the American Heart Association.

The "bottom line" is a set of chilling statistics from the National Heart, Lung, and Blood Institute:

- Heavy smokers are two to four times more likely to have a heart attack than nonsmokers.

- The heart-attack death rate among all smokers is 70 percent greater than that of nonsmokers.

- Older male smokers are nearly twice as likely to die from stroke as older men who do not smoke, and these odds are nearly as high for older female smokers.

- The risk of dying from lung cancer is 22 times higher for male smokers than for male nonsmokers and 12 times higher for female smokers than for female nonsmokers.

What's the Risk from Secondhand Smoke?

Nonsmokers exposed to someone else's smoke face a 25 percent greater risk of heart disease than those who live and work in smoke-free environments.[4] Researchers in Finland found that as little as 30 minutes in a smoke-filled room caused test subjects to lose blood stores of antioxidants such as vitamin C. It also causes LDL levels to rise. "We found that a short period of passive smoking changed cholesterol metabolism, favoring progression of atherosclerosis," says one of the study's authors, Timo Kuusi. "The cardiovascular system is extremely sensitive to the chemicals in environmental tobacco smoke," he says.[5]

Why Do African-Americans Face a Greater Risk of Heart Disease than Caucasians?

That's what the experts want to know, and some answers are starting to emerge. In 1999, Jackson State University and Tougaloo College teamed up with the University of Mississippi to begin a large-scale study of that question. The Jackson Heart Study is similar to the famous Framingham Study. In that Massachusetts town, scientists tracked people's habits and health status over more than 50 years. The Framingham study revealed most of what is known today about heart health and risks.

Herman Taylor, the director of the Mississippi study, says that African-Americans in his state lead the nation in deaths from heart disease and stroke. Their numbers have been increasing at the same time that other populations have shown declines. He hopes this research will uncover some reasons and point to ways to reverse that trend.

Getting answers from the Mississippi study will take time, but investigators have some ideas to start from. Some researchers think, for example, that inherited differences in body chemistry play a part. For example, scientists at the University of Georgia studied leg veins from patients who had bypass operations. They found that African-Americans make almost twice as many free radicals in their blood vessels as Caucasians do.

That finding is important to everyone, regardless of race. Free radicals are charged molecules that circulate in the bloodstream. They combine easily with oxygen and do a lot of damage. They prevent blood vessels from relaxing. Constricted arteries slow blood flow and raise blood pressure. Free radicals may also start the damage to artery walls that initiates plaque buildup. If these ideas hold up in further research, researchers may be able to develop antioxidant treatments. Such treatments would benefit all people.

What's Cholesterol, and What's So Bad About It?

Cholesterol has a worse reputation than it deserves. This waxy lipid (a kind of fat) is essential to good health. It builds the membranes that hold cells together. It's used in making certain hormones and bile, a digestive fluid. It's also part of the protective covering that wraps nerve fibers. Cholesterol is bad only when it forms plaques that block arteries and impede blood flow.

On the average, the liver manufactures about 80 percent of the body's cholesterol. Only about 20 percent comes from animal foods in the diet, such as meat, milk, eggs, butter, and others.[6] Because people vary in their genetic makeup, some make more cholesterol, regardless of diet. Others absorb more or less from food. For example, researchers at Wake Forest University found that about 15 percent of us have a gene called apo A-IV-2. People with this gene absorb less cholesterol from their food than those who carry the apo A-IV-1 variant.[7]

What's the Difference Between "Good Cholesterol" and "Bad Cholesterol?"

The cholesterol molecule does not dissolve in plasma. It circulates attached to water-soluble compounds called "lipoproteins." LDLs, for *low-d*ensity *l*ipoproteins, are the "bad" carriers. *High-d*ensity *l*ipoproteins, HDLs, are the so-called "good" carriers. So the cholesterol itself is no different, only the molecule it rides on.

LDLs are the "bad guys" because they carry cholesterol all around the body. They let it attach to artery walls. If it combines with oxygen there, it attracts white blood cells to the site. The body treats a buildup of oxidized LDL cholesterol as an injury. The area becomes inflamed, then heals, only to become inflamed and heal again. That sets the stage for a blood clot or heart attack.

Why are HDLs good? They carry cholesterol away from artery walls. They take it to the liver for disposal. They also prevent free radicals from combining with oxygen and damaging artery walls. "They're like little Pac-Men snarfing up the bad cholesterol—LDLs," says cardiologist Jack Davis, of Kalispell, Montana.

When doctors measure cholesterol levels, they look at the total amount of cholesterol in the blood, but they also compare HDLs and LDLs.

If My Cholesterol Is Too High, How Can I Reduce It?

Levels of blood cholesterol can be lowered by eating less fats of all kinds, eating fewer foods from animals, exercising, losing weight, and taking drugs to lower cholesterol (if prescribed by a physician).

Another way is to eat more foods rich in soluble fiber. The fiber traps cholesterol in the intestine and moves it out of the body. Four to six servings daily of citrus fruits (especially their white inner rind), apples, berries, carrots, dates, figs, prunes, cabbage, brussels sprouts, beans, lentils, peas, or sweet potatoes can lower cholesterol levels by as much as ten percent.

Oats, barley, rye, and other whole grains also deserve their reputation as cholesterol-busters. They are high in soluble fiber. They help

RISK CATEGORY	TOTAL CHOLESTEROL	LDL (BAD CHOLESTEROL)
	Measured in milligrams per deciliter.	
Low risk	Less than 200	Less than 130
Moderate risk	200–239	130–159
High risk	More than 240	More than 160

control blood sugar levels and prevent harmful substances from entering the bloodstream from the digestive system. The insoluble fibers in wheat and rice have disease-preventing benefits as well.

For many people, a diet low in fat helps reduce LDLs. Limiting luncheon meats, fatty beef, poultry skin, whole-milk products, cheese, butter, candy, bakery treats, and fried foods is probably a good idea for most of us. For anyone older than two, low-fat substitutes—such as skim milk for whole milk—are also a good idea.

"Interestingly, the individuals who seem to benefit most from cholesterol-lowering effects of a low-fat diet are those who are at the worst

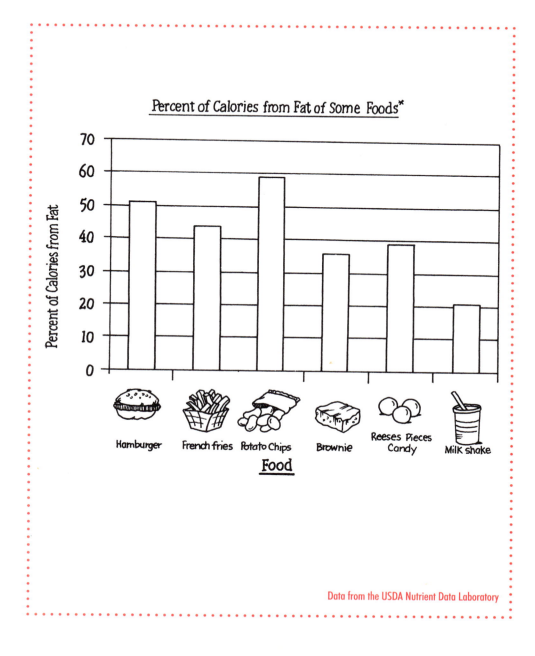

Percent of Calories from Fat of Some Foods*

Percent of Calories from Fat

Food

Hamburger · French fries · Potato Chips · Brownie · Reeses Pieces Candy · Milk shake

Data from the USDA Nutrient Data Laboratory

risk for heart attack and stroke," says Valentin Fuster of the American Heart Association. Research has also shown that physical activity works together with a low-fat diet to reduce LDLs. "Exercise and diet should be paired," Fuster says.[8]

Can Diet Prevent Heart Attacks and Strokes? No doubt about it. Besides not smoking and getting plenty of exercise, choosing the right foods and eating the right amounts are probably the most heart healthy habits you can adopt. The trouble is, you hear and read so much about eating healthfully that it's easy to get confused. In 1999, specialists in heart, cancer, child health, and nutrition got together with representatives from the National Institutes of Health. They ended the confusion by issuing a single set of guidelines to cover prevention of all major illnesses. [9]

"The good news is that we don't need one diet to prevent heart disease, another to decrease cancer risk, and yet another to prevent obesity and diabetes," says Richard Deckelbaum, a New York physician. "A single healthy diet cuts across disease categories to lower the risk of many chronic conditions," he adds.

The rest of the good news is that the guidelines are simple and rather easy to follow. If your health is good, you don't smoke at all or drink much, and you keep your weight at a healthy level, these guidelines may be all you need to reduce your risk of major illness. Of course, infants, pregnant women, the elderly, and people with health problems may need to follow special diets their doctors recommend. But for most of us, the advice is simple:

- Eat a variety of foods.

- Choose most foods from plant sources.

- Eat five or more servings of fruits and vegetables daily.

- Eat six or more servings daily of whole-grain bread, cereals, rice, or pasta.

- Limit foods high in fat or cholesterol, particularly those from animal sources.

- Avoid foods high in sugar.

Plant foods in general contain many substances that are important to health maintenance and disease prevention. In addition to vitamins and minerals, plant foods contain phytic acid and phenolic acid. Those chemicals are antioxidants. They slow the rate at which oxygen combines with free radicals. Antioxidants include the vitamins A, C, and E in yellow and green vegetables, tomatoes, citrus fruits, and other plant foods. There's another benefit to fruits and vegetables. Those rich in potassium, such as bananas, oranges, and leafy greens, also help prevent high blood pressure.

How can you tell a whole-grain bread, cereal, or pasta product? Check the label. If the first ingredient is listed as "whole wheat," "whole-grain wheat," or "whole-grain oats," you are probably making a good choice. Be careful. Dark breads aren't necessarily whole grain, and too much sugar (look for sucrose, corn syrup, dextrose, and fructose on the label) may ruin a cereal.

Avoiding too much fat is important for several reasons. Cholesterol in fatty foods contributes directly to the buildup of plaque in arteries, but fatty foods have indirect effects, too. Even one high-fat meal can trigger blood clotting, the American Heart Association warns. Danish researcher Lone Frost Larsen found that levels and activity of Factor VIIa, a clotting factor, rose 60 percent after a high-fat meal—even in healthy young people who had no signs of heart disease.[10]

If a Diet Low in Fats Is Good for Me, Isn't a Very Low Fat or No-Fat Diet Even Better? No. Your body needs some fats for growth and development as well as for its everyday functioning. A target of about 30 percent of daily Calories from fat is probably about right for most people. Calories measure the energy in food. That means if you consume 2,500 Calories a day, no more than 750 of them should come from fat. That may sound like a lot, but at nine Calories a gram, fat Calories can add up fast. The key is not to avoid all fats, but to get the balance right.

Too much fat suppresses your body's ability to fight disease. But so may too little, especially if you are physically active. David Pendergast, at the University of Buffalo, studied competitive runners. He found that those who increased the proportion of fat in their diets from 17 to 32 percent of their daily calories improved their endurance. They suffered no negative effects in weight, body composition, pulse rate, or total cholesterol. He also found higher levels of disease-fighting white cells and lower levels of inflammatory chemicals in their blood.

A diet too low in fat deprives the body of important nutrients. U.S. Department of Agriculture surveys show that more than half of women who reduce their fat intake to less than 30 percent of Calories fail to get enough vitamin A, vitamin E, folic acid, calcium, iron, or zinc.[11] Such deficiencies increase the risk of osteoporosis ("brittle-bone disease"), cancer, and problems during pregnancy.

Experts agree that almost everyone over the age of two can benefit from eating less fat, regardless of the kind. Not all fats are created equal, however. The difference has to do with hydrogen atoms that bond to the fat molecules. The greater the number of hydrogens, the more "saturated" the fat is said to be. Here's the rundown:

- The *saturated* fats in meats, full-fat dairy products, and butter raise cholesterol levels.

- The hardening of vegetable oils into margarine, achieved by adding hydrogens, creates *trans-fatty acids*. Some experts think they may pose as great a risk as the saturated fats in animal foods.

- The *polyunsaturated* fats of most liquid vegetable oils and fish are safer for the heart and blood. *In small amounts*, they reduce both total cholesterol and LDLs ("bad cholesterol").

- *Monounsaturated* fatty acids in some oils help maintain levels of HDLs, the "good cholesterol." They may also protect nerve cells in the brain.

- *Omega-3 fatty acids* in certain fish, fish oils, flaxseed oil, and some plants may help prevent disorders ranging from heart disease to depression. In addition to lowering cholesterol, they prevent clotting by reducing the stickiness of platelets.

Still confused? Keep your total fat consumption at reasonable levels and follow this thumbs-up, thumbs-down guide:

FAT	FOUND IN	RATING
Cholesterol	Animal foods, especially whole milk, cream, and organ meats such as liver and tongue	👎
Saturated fats	Butter, red meat, poultry skin, chocolate, shortening, cheese, whole milk, coconut and palm oils	👎
Trans-fatty acids	Hard margarine, baked goods, packaged snacks, fried foods, fast foods	👎
Monounsaturated fats	Canola, olive, and nut oils	👍 IN SMALL AMOUNTS
Polyunsaturated fats	Fish and most vegetable oils (except palm and coconut)	👍 IN SMALL AMOUNTS
Omega-3 fatty acids	Fatty fish, such as tuna or salmon	👍 IN SMALL AMOUNTS

One other food merits consideration. Sugars aren't fats. They are carbohydrates, but the amount of fat in the bloodstream rises even more than it normally would when fat and sugar are eaten together. The American College of Nutrition measured fat in the blood of people who (1) drank a fatty milkshake sweetened with sugar or (2) drank a milkshake made with the same amount of fat but no sugar. Over the next eight hours, blood fats ran 38 to 60 percent higher with the sugar-sweetened shakes. "Sugars lead to high fat levels," the study concluded.

Does It Matter What I Eat While I'm Young?

"As a society, we are digging our own graves with our forks and spoons," says Mayo Clinic cardiologist Brooks Edwards.[12]

His message extends to people of all ages and nationalities, as some scientists learned when they compared Japanese young people, ages six to 15, with Australians and Americans of the same age. They found that the Japanese children, on the average, have higher HDL ("good cholesterol") levels, and their HDLs decline less with age. Japanese children get more exercise and eat less fat. They also eat more soybean products. (Soybeans contain plant hormones that retard the absorption of cholesterol into the blood from the intestine.) The scientists think the comparisons may explain why Americans and Australians are five times more likely to die of heart disease than the Japanese.[13]

Another study of people between the ages of 12 and 16 in Taiwan found that high blood pressure, diabetes, and high LDL levels went along with obesity. Approximately 70 percent of obese boys had one of these risk factors, and 25 percent had two or more.[14] "This was a significant finding," says Nain-Feng Chu, one of the authors of the study, "as the cardiovascular disease rate is increasing in Taiwan due to the growing availability of a high-fat, high-energy diet and an increasingly sedentary lifestyle."

Do Vitamins and Minerals Help the Heart?

Vitamins are essential to good health. They are important for growth, digestion, and mental and nerve functions. They enhance the immune system's ability to fight off infection. They enable cells to break down and use the carbohydrates, fats, and proteins present in food. You don't get energy from vitamins, but you can't use the energy in food without them.

Of the 13 vitamins we know about, four are stored in body fat. They are vitamins A, D, E, and K. The other nine dissolve in water, so you excrete them in urine rather than storing them in the body. These are vitamin C and the eight B vitamins: thiamine (B-1); riboflavin (B-2); niacin, B-6, pantothenic acid, B-12, biotin, and folic acid.

In addition, your body needs 15 minerals used in building cells, making them work, or both. The quantities you need are very small—usually measured in millionths or thousandths of grams. You need tiny amounts of chromium, copper, fluorine, iodine, iron, manganese, molybdenum, selenium, zinc, chloride, potassium, and sodium. You need relatively larger amounts of calcium, phosphorus, and magnesium.

Among the thousands of chemical reactions that occur inside living cells, it's hard to sort out exactly what any single vitamin or mineral does. Table 3 on page 153 suggests a few associations that are known or presumed.

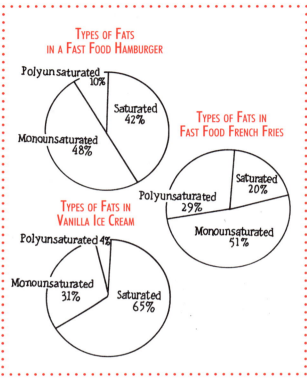

TYPES OF FATS IN A FAST FOOD HAMBURGER
Polyunsaturated 10%
Saturated 42%
Monounsaturated 48%

TYPES OF FATS IN FAST FOOD FRENCH FRIES
Saturated 20%
Polyunsaturated 29%
Monounsaturated 51%

TYPES OF FATS IN VANILLA ICE CREAM
Polyunsaturated 4%
Monounsaturated 31%
Saturated 65%

Should I Take Vitamin or Mineral Supplements?

The American Dietetic Association, the National Academy of Sciences, and a number of other major medical societies agree: Healthy people can get all the vitamins and minerals they need from a balanced diet. Real food is better than pills, these experts say, because it provides important trace elements that pills don't.

On the other hand, most people fail to eat properly, at least some of the time. For example, only one person in ten eats the five servings of fruits and vegetables recommended daily.[15] A Michigan State University study reports that four out of five young people in the United States fail to get the minimum requirements of calcium, iron, and zinc from their diets. As many as one in five of us faces an increased risk of heart attack and stroke because we do not get enough B vitamins.[16] Therefore, some doctors believe that a single, balanced multivitamin and mineral capsule a day won't do any harm and might just help.

But all the experts agree that it's not smart to start popping pills just because of something that you see in a newspaper or magazine or on television. "We aren't suggesting people take more than a multivitamin," says New York researcher Richard Benson.

Why Is Exercise Good for the Heart?

Linger on that couch watching your favorite sitcoms, and you face a risk of heart disease six times greater than the active person does.[17] Get out and walk, climb stairs, cycle, or dance for an hour a day, and you cut your stroke risk almost in half.[18]

Exercise strengthens the heart, making it more efficient with each beat. It helps keep weight at normal levels and relieves stress. It decreases plaque formation on artery walls. Some studies have found exercise more effective than drugs in lowering blood pressure and preventing heart attacks.

In addition, exercise . . .

- prevents the development of high blood pressure.

- decreases total cholesterol and LDLs and increases HDLs.

- prevents irregularities in heartbeat rhythm and rate.

- improves the ability of artery linings to produce nitric oxide, which causes vessels to relax and contract more efficiently.

- prevents blood clots.

Regular, moderate exercise from childhood into old age protects the circulatory system better than occasional workouts or programs started late in life. The summer softball player who gets no exercise in the winter enjoys fewer benefits, for example, than the walker who's active in every season.

Does Exercise Make the Heart Beat Faster or Slower?

Both. Heart rate increases during exercise, but the resting rate decreases as you become more fit. Why? Because the heart, like any muscle, gets stronger with use.

To grow stronger, the heart must pump harder and faster. Activities such as soccer, basketball, tennis, running, fast dancing, stair climbing, fast walking, swimming, or cycling qualify. A stronger heart gives more push to more blood with each contraction. Therefore, it can beat more slowly during quiet times and still deliver all the oxygen the body requires. Adults who exercise frequently often boast resting heart rates of 40 to 60 beats a minute, much slower than the average of about 60 to 80 for less-fit people. The hearts of fit individuals also speed up less during exercise, because their hearts are more efficient. They pump more blood with each beat.

Weight training, once thought ineffective in promoting heart health, has now been shown to have benefits. According to the American Heart Association, it decreases cholesterol levels, lowers blood pressure, and reduces body fat.

Why Do Experts Recommend Training at a Certain Pulse Rate, and Why Does the Number Go Down for Older People?

The answer is part physical, part psychological.

First, the heart's maximum beat rate diminishes over the years. A child's heart can beat as fast as 220 times a minute during strenuous play, but by age 20, the maximum begins to drop by one beat a year. By age 30, the heart produces less of a protein that regulates how long each beat lasts. The heart must work harder with each beat to keep up its normal output. A quick way to estimate the maximum is to subtract age in years from 220.

Second, studies have shown that aerobic or cardiovascular exercise—activity that strengthens the circulatory system—is most effective within the range of 60 and 90 percent of the maximum pulse rate. Exercising at the lower end of that range decreases body fat, blood pressure, and the amount of cholesterol in the blood. Workouts at the upper end increase the size and number of blood vessels, the capacity of the lungs, and the heart's stroke volume (the amount of blood pumped per beat).

Finally, the recommended range takes into account those all-important matters of attitude, willpower, and stick-to-itiveness. Exercise too slowly, and you'll get bored. Work out too hard, and you'll become tired, cross, and injury-prone.

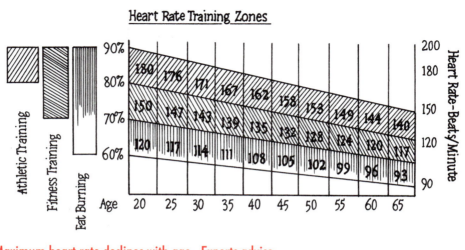

Heart Rate Training Zones

Maximum heart rate declines with age. Experts advise training within the 60% to 90% training range.

How Much Exercise Is Enough?

If you sit at a desk all day, spend most of your leisure time watching TV or sleeping, and seldom work up a sweat, you probably already know you need to exercise more. But if you wait tables, stock groceries, or spend a lot of time walking, dancing, or doing yard work, you may not be so sure.

The American Heart Association says that four hours a day of hard physical labor, such as digging or loading heavy boxes, puts you in the highly active category. Cycling, jogging, or swimming for 30 to 60 minutes at least three times a week does the same. Walking that is brisk enough to get your heart rate up qualifies too, if you do it for an hour a day four or more days of the week. Even a half-hour a day of moderately brisk walking has heart-protective effects.

But you needn't be a jock to protect your heart with exercise. Even moderate activity has benefits. A 1999 study of men in the Honolulu Heart Program found that walking only two miles a day cut their risk of heart attack in half, as compared with men who walked less than one-quarter mile per day.[19] When's a good time to start walking? "We should become active as early in life as possible," says Robert Abbott, of the University of Virginia, one of the authors of the study. "The earlier we start, the easier it is to continue those habits later in life."

How Strenuous Does Exercise Need to Be to Benefit the Heart?

Forget, "No pain, no gain." The American College of Sports Medicine says you'll do your body just as much good walking at 2.5 miles per hour for forty minutes as you will walking at 3.8 miles per hour for 30 minutes. Also, if exercising hasn't been a habit, choose activities that reduce the risk of injury, such as swimming or cycling, over weight-bearing activities, such as running or high-impact aerobics. Workouts needn't be lengthy either. The American Heart Association says three ten-minute sweat-breaking sessions may be just as good as a single 30-minute one. The critical variable is frequency of exercise—doing something active at least three or four days a week.

Should I Eat Before Exercising or Competing in an Athletic Event?

Probably not. When food is in the stomach, the cardiovascular system sends more blood into the digestive organs, boosting their action. An empty stomach triggers a partial shutdown of blood flow to digestive organs. That makes extra blood available to the arms and legs, which may mean that your muscles will work better whether you are doing step aerobics or playing football. It also means that you will avoid the stomach cramps that can occur when exercise deprives the digestive system of an adequate blood supply. Experts say to wait at least an hour after a meal before exercising, and don't forget to drink plenty of water before, during, and after your workout.

Does Drinking Red Wine Prevent Heart Attacks?

It's going to take a long time to settle that controversy. Some researchers have concluded that small amounts of *any* alcoholic beverage increase HDLs and decrease LDLs and clotting. In one study, light drinkers—those who consumed an average of one beer or one small glass of wine daily—cut their risk of blocked arteries to the brain in half.[20] In another, they reduced their risk of a second heart attack by 20 to 30 percent.[21]

But not all research yields the same results. Other studies find benefits in wine, but not in beer or distilled liquors. Some experts think that wine is superior because it contains antioxidants that inhibit the activity of free radicals. If that's the reason, there's nothing special about wine. Grape juice and many other fruits and vegetables contain just as many antioxidants.

Still other studies find no benefits in any alcoholic drink. English researchers have reported that while the French—who consume more red wine—suffer heart disease far less frequently than the English, they die in greater numbers from alcohol-related diseases. They also point out that the incidence of heart disease in France is rising as the French consume more foods that are fatty.

Also, alcohol drinkers face an increased risk of stroke. A study of men in Scotland showed that those who consume three or more drinks a day die younger than moderate drinkers do. Heavy drinkers doubled their risk of stroke.[22] Italian and Austrian researchers reported that drinking more than 3.5 ounces (100 grams) of alcohol per day (roughly equal to four bottles of beer) produced an even greater risk of stroke than smoking a pack of cigarettes daily.[23]

It's well known that alcohol consumption exceeding one or two drinks daily damages the heart muscle, produces abnormal rhythms, and increases the risk of sudden cardiac death. For these and other obvious reasons, doctors are reluctant to advise their patients to drink alcohol. "In the United States, heavy alcohol consumption is a leading cause of avoidable deaths," says Charles Hennekens, Professor of Medicine at Harvard University.

So, until the researchers sort out all the variables, common sense prevails. An occasional glass of wine or beer probably does little harm to adults who enjoy it, but there's no reason to take up drinking for health's sake.

Can Aspirin Prevent Heart Attacks and Strokes?

Doctors sometimes prescribe a baby aspirin daily for heart patients. Aspirin is an anticlotting drug. It can dissolve clots after they form or prevent them from forming in the first place. How? By combating inflammation.

Normally, inflammation is a good sign. The swelling, redness, pain, heat, and stiffness that accompany an injury or irritation let you know that your immune system is at work fighting infection. But the immune system can sometimes "get it wrong" and attack healthy tissue. Where plaque blocks an artery, inflammation can weaken the vessel further. It can irritate the plaque and cause rupturing or clotting. Aspirin interferes with the inflammatory process and reduces the risk of heart attack, especially among elderly people, who are most likely to form blood clots.

Do Birth-Control Pills Increase the Chance of Heart Attacks and Strokes?

Thirty years of research have shown that women worry far more about the risks of birth-control pills than they need to, especially the low-dose varieties. Women who have a history of blood clots should not take the Pill. Neither should smokers or women with liver disease. Those with diabetes, high blood pressure, high cholesterol, or a family history of heart disease should talk to their doctors before making a decision.

For those outside these categories, the risk of heart attack runs around two in 10,000. (It's one in 10,000 for those who don't take the Pill.) Stroke risk is very small, but women over 50 who have taken the Pill for five years or less in their lifetimes have slightly higher blood pressures.[24]

What Can I Do to Prevent Heart Disease?

Think ahead. If you are young and healthy, you may find it hard to believe that you'll ever be 30 someday, much less 40, 50, or 60. You realize that other people get sick and die, but it is hard to imagine anything happening to you. But it's a fact that no one stays forever young, no matter what you see in the movies. You wouldn't play tag in the middle of a busy freeway, would you? You'd recognize the risk. Use that same common sense when you think about long-term risks such as cigarette smoking, poor food choices, and lack of exercise.

First, don't smoke. If you smoke now, quit immediately. The less time you have smoked, the better your chances that your body can repair the damage that has been done. If you don't smoke, don't start, and don't hang out with people who smoke or in smoky places. Secondhand smoke is just as deadly as the smoker's own.

Second, watch what you eat. Although no foods are "bad foods," too many foods high in fat or sugar and low in nutrients can clog arteries with plaque. Excess weight strains the heart, while diets too low in essential vitamins and minerals starve body cells and disrupt blood chemistry.

Third, get up and moving. Exercise today. Exercise every day. Physical activity and a sensible diet lower cholesterol and help control blood pressure. Exercise is also a great mood elevator.

Finally, control stress in your life. Find ways of dealing with the frustrations that are a normal part of living. Avoid situations that set your blood boiling, whether it's rush-hour traffic or long lines at the post office. When anger comes on, take deep breaths, count to ten, and work to achieve calmer, happier feelings. Talk things over with a friend or counselor. Release frustrations through physical exercise. Exert your sense of humor. A good laugh improves circulation and oxygen exchange and enhances your immune system. Spend happy times with those you love. Your heart—and your mind—will thank you for it.

Test Your Heart Smarts

· · · · ·

Here the heart may give a useful lesson to the head.

William Cowper

· · · · ·

How heart smart are you? The National Heart, Lung, and Blood Institute wants you to know.[25] Record your true-false answers on a piece of paper. Then check them against the answers that follow these 20 statements.

- Score 17 or more and you can count yourself as five-star heart smart.
- Score 13–16 and you're on your way, but there's more you need to learn.
- Score 12 or below? Don't wait. Call 1-800-575-WELL, or visit the institute's website at http://www.nhlbi.nih.gov.

TRUE or *FALSE*?
1. The risk factors for heart disease that you can do something about are high blood pressure, high blood cholesterol, smoking, obesity, and physical inactivity.

TRUE or *FALSE*?
2. The symptoms of high blood pressure and high blood cholesterol are chest pains and shortness of breath.

TRUE or *FALSE*?
3. A blood pressure greater than or equal to 140/90 (measured in millimeters of mercury) is generally considered high.

TRUE or *FALSE*?
4. A blood cholesterol level of 240 mg/dL (milligrams per deciliter) is desirable for adults.

TRUE or *FALSE*?
5. Eating foods low in cholesterol is the best way to lower blood cholesterol.

TRUE or *FALSE*?
6. People under the age of 20 don't need to get their blood cholesterol checked.

TRUE or *FALSE*?
7. Smoking causes lung cancer and heart disease, but is not a risk factor for strokes.

TRUE or *FALSE*?
8. Heart disease is the leading killer of both men and women in the United States.

TRUE or *FALSE*?
9. The best way to lower cholesterol is to quit eating red meat.

TRUE or *FALSE*?
10. Fish-oil supplements are good for lowering cholesterol.

TRUE or *FALSE*?
11. Saturated fats raise the blood cholesterol level more than anything else in food.

TRUE or *FALSE*?
12. All vegetable oils help lower blood cholesterol levels.

Nutritionists say 3 ounces is an adequate serving size for meat. How does that amount compare with the 16-ounce steak-house T-bone?

TRUE or *FALSE*?
13. Regular physical activity can reduce your chances of getting heart disease.

TRUE or *FALSE*?
14. Most people get enough physical activity from their normal daily routine.

TRUE or *FALSE*?
15. You need to train hard for at least an hour a day to get physically fit.

TRUE or *FALSE*?
16. People who maintain a healthy weight don't need to exercise.

TRUE or *FALSE*?
17. All forms of exercise have the same benefits for the heart and circulatory system.

TRUE or *FALSE*?
18. Young people need less exercise than older people.

TRUE or *FALSE*?
19. Anyone who starts a diet or exercise program should consult a doctor first.

TRUE or *FALSE*?
20. People who have had heart attacks should not exercise.

Answers

1. *TRUE*. You can't change your sex, age, or family history, but you can work on your diet, smoking habits, and exercise.

2. *FALSE*. A person with high blood pressure or high blood cholesterol may feel fine and look great, unaware of any problem until a stroke or heart attack occurs. Heart smart people get regular checkups that include blood pressure measurements and a blood test for cholesterol.

3. *TRUE*. A blood pressure of 140/90 (measured in millimeters of mercury) or greater is generally classified as high blood pressure. However, blood pressures that fall below 140/90 can sometimes be a problem. A diastolic pressure (the second number) between 85–89 increases the risk for heart disease and stroke. People in this category should have their blood pressure checked at least once a year by a health professional.

4. *FALSE*. A blood cholesterol level of 240 mg/dL (milligrams per deciliter) or above is high, and increases the risk of heart disease. If total cholesterol exceeds

200, most doctors look carefully at more sensitive measures that compare LDLs and HDLs. A high level of LDL cholesterol increases the risk for heart disease, as does a low level of HDL cholesterol.

5. *FALSE*. Cutting cholesterol intake can help, but the body makes cholesterol from any fats available. That's why limiting all fats in the diet, especially saturated fats, is the best strategy.

6. *FALSE*. Children and teens from "high risk" families, in which a parent has high blood cholesterol or in which a parent or grandparent has had heart disease at an early age (at 55 years of age or younger), should have their cholesterol levels tested. After age 20, everyone regardless of family history should have a blood cholesterol check at least every five years.

7. *FALSE*. Smoking is a major risk factor for four of the five leading causes of death, including heart attack, stroke, cancer, and lung diseases such as emphysema and bronchitis.

8. *TRUE*. Coronary heart disease killed 476,124 Americans in 1996. That's nearly one in every five deaths.[26] It's the number one killer of both men and women.

9. *FALSE*. Although some red meat is high in saturated fat and cholesterol, red meat is also an important source of protein, iron, and other vitamins and minerals. Choose lean cuts with the fat trimmed away, and eat a reasonable amount. Experts define a serving as three ounces. That's about the size of a single deck of playing cards.

10. *TRUE* or *FALSE*. Trick question! Give yourself a point whatever you answered. Some research suggests that fish-oil supplements reduce blood cholesterol. Other studies show no effect. However, everyone agrees that fish is a good food choice, because it's low in saturated fat.

11. *TRUE*. These fats are found in largest amounts in animal products such as butter, cheese, whole milk, ice cream, cream, and fatty meats. They are also found in some vegetable oils—coconut, palm, and palm-kernel oils.

12. *FALSE*. Most vegetable oils—canola, corn, olive, safflower, soybean, and sunflower oils—contain mostly monounsaturated and polyunsaturated fats, which help lower blood cholesterol when used in place of saturated fats. However, a few vegetable oils—coconut, palm, and palm-kernel oils—contain more saturated fat than unsaturated fat. Also, the hardening of vegetable oils into margarine forms trans-fatty acids.

13. *TRUE*. Regular physical activity (even mild to moderate exercise) reduces risk.

14. *FALSE*. Most people are busy but not active.

15. *FALSE*. Even 30 minutes of moderate physical activity daily can help improve heart health and lower the risk of heart disease.

16. *FALSE*. Everyone needs exercise regardless of weight.

17. *FALSE*. The exercise needn't be strenuous, but it must increase your heart rate. Stretching and weight lifting increase flexibility and muscle strength without cardiovascular benefits.

18. *FALSE*. Everyone needs exercise, regardless of age.

19. *TRUE*. Talk to your doctor before you change your diet or exercise routine.

20. *FALSE*. Regular physical activity reduces the risk of a second heart attack.

• • • • •

In Closing

In the new world the most important thing to
know is what you don't know.

• RICHARD SMITH •

What have you thought about as you read the questions and answers on these pages? Perhaps the unfailing durability of the circulatory system impressed you. That unassuming circuit of pumps and pipes quietly sees most people through their allotted "three score and ten"—whether mountaineer or musician, pirate or poet.

Maybe you thought about the system's amazing adaptability. In most cases, it works flawlessly whether its owner runs marathons or snoozes away the afternoon.

If you're chemistry-minded, you may have wondered at the thousands of chemical reactions required to maintain the blood and body fluids. Imagine all those atoms and molecules moving, changing, combining, and recombining in the intricate sequences that sustain life. Their dance is more complex than any human choreographer could ever imagine.

Perhaps you thought most about the health of your body and your commitment to maintain and preserve it. Exercising and eating right are as essential to your survival as the air you breathe and the water you drink.

Maybe you considered the science of it all. How many men and women worldwide labor daily to wrest nature's secrets from her? Thousands, certainly. Millions, perhaps. They know that learning is never easy, but they press on, undeterred. Knowledge is elusive, and so much remains unknown and undiscovered. But that's always the way with science, isn't it? The questions keep coming. The more we learn, the more there is to know.

Our exploration of inner space is not so different from our probings of the solar system and the universe beyond. We have a general idea of the territory, but we must travel farther and farther from the familiar to get the closer looks we need. Every year, our investigative tools improve, and our observations take us deeper into the unknown. The frontiers of health and medicine are not distant stars and galaxies, but our own life processes. We survive—even thrive—because of forces we discern only dimly. We turn our telescopes inward even as we turn them outward, searching not only for answers, but for the questions we know too little to ask.

We started this book with Helen Welshimer's advice: "It would be a splendid plan to take a walk around yourself." If this walk has been pleasant or instructive or stimulating, perhaps you are ready for a longer journey.

Read.

Think.

Ask questions.

Investigate.

Explore the universe within you.

Table 1
SOME ENDOCRINE GLANDS AND THEIR PRODUCTS AND ACTIONS

GLAND	HORMONE	ACTION
Anterior pituitary: "master gland"	FSH: Follicle stimulating hormone	Causes the reproductive organs to produce sex hormones (in both males and females)
	LH: Leutenizing hormone	Causes release of egg from ovary (in women) and production of testosterone (a male hormone) in both sexes
	GH: Growth hormone	Regulates growth process
	Prolactin	Controls development, growth, and milk production by mammary glands
	TSH: Thyroid stimulating hormone	Stimulates the thyroid to produce thyroxine
	ACTH: Adrenocorticotropic hormone	Stimulates the adrenal glands to produce steroid hormones
	ICSH: Interstitial cell stimulating hormone	Causes the reproductive organs to produce sex hormones (in both males and females)
	MSH: Melanin stimulating hormone	Causes the skin to darken (melanin production in response to sunlight)
	LPH: Lipotropic hormone	Moves fat out of fatty tissues
Hypothalamus	Oxytocin (stored in the posterior pituitary)	In females, the ejection of milk, expulsion of eggs, and contraction of the uterus; also causes milk flow from breasts
	Vasopressin (also stored in the posterior pituitary)	Raises blood pressure; prevents the kidneys from excreting too much water (retains water in body)

Table 1 (continued)

GLAND	HORMONE	ACTION
Ovaries (in females)	Estrogen	Growth and development of reproductive organs
Ovaries (in females)	Progesterone	Prepares body for pregnancy; maintains pregnancy
Testes (in males)	Androgens (any of several male hormones)	Growth and development of reproductive system
Thyroid	Thyroxine	Regulates metabolism (extraction of energy from food)
	Calcitonin	Along with parathyroid hormone, controls body's calcium level
Parathyroid	Parathyroid hormone	Regulates calcium level in the body (important to bone structure and muscle and nerve functions)
Adrenal medulla (inner part of the adrenal gland)	Epinephrine (adrenaline) and norepinephrine (noradrenaline)	Raise blood pressure; accelerate heart rate; increase blood glucose; control "fight-or-flight" body preparedness for emergencies
Adrenal cortex (outer part of the adrenal gland)	Steroid hormones: cortisone and aldosterone	Regulate fluid and electrolyte (salt) balance
Pancreas (islets of Langerhans cells)	Insulin and glucagon	Keep blood sugar (glucose) in a normal range

Table 2
THE CELLS OF THE IMMUNE SYSTEM

Although all are white blood cells (leukocytes), nearly all work outside the blood stream in the body tissues, as well as in the blood.

NAME	MISSION
Stem cells	Located primarily in the bone marrow; "parents" of all blood cells, including leukocytes.
Phagocytes, including monocytes, macrophages, and dendritic cells	Consume invaders and display their antigens on cell membrane. The display attracts T cells. Phagocytes also clean up dead cells and debris. Dendritic cells are important regulators of immune functions.
Granulocytes, including neutrophils, eosinophils, basophils, and mast cells	Perform many different functions, from releasing enzymes that kill bacteria to combating worm parasites. Most are involved in inflammation and may also cause autoimmune disease.
B cells, plasma cells	B cells become plasma cells. Plasma cells manufacture antibodies specific to a single antigen.
Helper T cells (also called CD4 cells)	Inspect foreign proteins presented on cell surfaces; trigger antibody production by B cells.
Suppressor T cells	Regulate immune response by decreasing antibody production.
Killer T cells (also called CD8 cells or cytotoxic T cells)	Destroy cancer cells and cells infected with viruses; also play a major part in rejection of transplanted organs.
Natural killer cells	Dissolve membranes of abnormal cells. Along with killer T cells, NKs are powerful weapons against cancer cells and cells infected with viruses.
Memory cells	Retain instructions for antibody production against previously encountered antigens; stored in lymph nodes.

Table 3
SOME VITAMINS AND MINERALS:
BENEFITS, CAUTIONS, AND SOURCES

VITAMIN OR MINERAL	POSSIBLE CARDIO-VASCULAR BENEFIT	POSSIBLE REASON	CAUTION! TOO MUCH MAY...	GOOD SOURCES
Vitamin A	None or minimal (disputed)	Antioxidant: hinders LDL oxidation (in test tube)	cause cancer or birth defects.	Carrots, liver, eggs, sweet potatoes, spinach, melons
Vitamins B_6, B_{12}, and folic acid	Reduced risk of heart disease or heart attack and stroke	Reduces levels of an amino acid, homocysteine, which may damage artery walls (disputed)	damage the nervous system.	Beans, nuts, seeds, liver, spinach, citrus fruits
Vitamin C	Slight reduction in heart disease risk (disputed)	Antioxidant: hinders LDL oxidation, reduces fats in blood, decreases clotting proteins, reduces ability of certain immune cells to bind to artery walls	cause diarrhea, stomach upset, and kidney stones.	Broccoli, citrus fruits, tomatoes, cabbage, peppers, berries, potatoes
Vitamin E	Reduced risk of coronary disease	Antioxidant: hinders LDL oxidation	interfere with platelet clumping essential to clotting.	Vegetable oils, wheat germ, nuts, cheese, some green vegetables, peanut butter, some cereals
Potassium	Lowers blood pressure	Promotes sodium excretion, dilates vessels, reduces sensitivity to hormones that raise blood pressure, improves nervous system's control of heart rate	cause muscle weakness, paralysis, heart attacks, convulsions.	Bananas, raisins, oranges, green leafy vegetables

Table 3 (continued)

VITAMIN OR MINERAL	POSSIBLE CARDIO-VASCULAR BENEFIT	POSSIBLE REASON	CAUTION! TOO MUCH MAY...	GOOD SOURCES
Iron	Prevents or treats certain forms of anemia	Used in building the hemoglobin molecule	increase risk of heart disease and cancer, especially in men and older women.	Red meat, chicken, seafood, green leafy vegetables, whole grains
Magnesium	Slight reduction in blood pressure; improves efficiency of oxygen use, which reduces strain on heart	Relaxes blood vessels	cause muscle weakness, lack of coordination, drowsiness, confusion, coma.	Onions, green peas, spinach, potatoes, peanut butter, tofu

NOTES

Chapter One

1. The Reader's Digest Association, Inc., *ABC's of the Human Body: A Family Answer Book* (Pleasantville, NY: Reader's Digest Association, 1987), p. 244.

2. Ibid., p. 245.

3. Ibid.

4. Ibid., p. 112.

5. Michael E. DeBakey and Antonio M. Gotto Jr., *The New Living Heart* (Holbrook, MA; Adams Media Corp., 1997), p. 43.

6. *World Book Encyclopedia of Science*, *The Human Body* Vol. 7 (Chicago: World Book, Inc, 1987), p. 20.

7. Neil Boyce, "Out for Blood: Cooking Up an Alternative to the Red Stuff Is Proving a Tough Task," *New Scientist*, November 29, 1997.

8. Alvin, Virginia, and Robert Silverstein, *The Circulatory System* (New York: Henry Holt, 1994), p. 52.

9. Lennart Nilsson, *The Body Victorious: The Illustrated Story of Our Immune System and Other Defenses of the Human Body* (New York: Delacorte, 1985), p. 63.

10. Regina Avraham, *The Circulatory System* (New York: Chelsea House, 1989), p. 13.

11. A., V., and R. Silverstein, *The Circulatory System*, p. 18.

12. Ibid., p. 43.

13. Ibid., p. 41. Other sources estimate as much as a minute.

14. DeBakey and Gotto, *The New Living Heart,* p. 17.

15. Ibid., p. 38.

16. Carol Ballard, *The Human Body: The Heart and Circulatory System* (Austin, Texas: Raintree Steck-Vaughn, 1997), p. 26.

17. A., V., and R. Silverstein, *The Circulatory System*, p. 38.

18. Ibid.

19. Carol A. Turkington and Jeffrey S. Dover, *Skin Deep: An A-Z of Skin Disorders, Treatment, and Health* (New York: Facts On File, 1996), p. 323.

20. Lynda Jones, "Summer Survival Guide," *Science World* (May 5, 1995), p. 17.

21. Reader's Digest Association, p. 260.

22. *The World Book Encyclopedia of Science,* p. 23. The Reader's Digest Association says 250 million.

23. A., V., and R. Silverstein, *The Circulatory System,* p. 51.

24. Ibid., p. 26.

25. S. Kurachi, Y. Deyashiki, J. Takeshita, and K. Kurachi, "Genetic Mechanisms of Age Regulation of Human Blood Coagulation Factor IX," *Science* (July 30, 1999).

26. Those seeking an in-depth exploration of this topic should consult Anthony Walsh, *The Science of Love: Understanding Love & Its Effects on Mind & Body* (Buffalo, NY: Prometheus Books, 1996).

27. Barrie Gillies, "The Love Buzz: Why You Get High," *Cosmopolitan,* (January 1998), p. 142.

28. Deborah Blum, "Dopamine: The Plunge of Pleasure," *Psychology Today,* (September-October 1997), p. 46.

29. Nuna Alberts, "The Science of Love," *Life* (February 1999), p. 42.

Chapter Two

1. Michael D. McGoon, ed., *Mayo Clinic Heart Book* (New York: William Morrow: 1993), p. 6.

2. A., W., and R. Silverstein, *The Circulatory System,* p. 37.

3. S. Kulkarni, I. O'Farrell, M. Erasi, and M.S. Kochar, "Stress and Hypertension," *Wisconsin Medical Journal* (December 1998), p. 34.

4. M. A. Mittleman, D. Mintzer, M. Maclure, G. Tofler, J. Sherwood, and J. Muller, "Triggering of Myocardial Infarction by Cocaine," *Circulation* (June 1, 1999).

5. "Smoking Pot Boosts Heart Attack Risk," United Press International, March 2, 2000.

6. Laura Helmuth, "Portrait of the Artery as a Motivator," *Science News* (May 8, 1999).

7. DeBakey and Gotto, *The New Living Heart*, p. 382.

8. American Heart Association, *1999 Heart and Stroke Statistical Update*, p. 26.

9. Dr. Jack Davis, Personal communication.

10. Jenny Bryan, *Body Talk: The Pulse of Life* (New York: Dillon Press, 1992), p. 38.

11. American Heart Association, 1999 Heart and Stroke Statistical Update, p. 26.

12. Ibid., p. 18.

13. Ibid., p. 26.

14. Charlotte Gray, "Just a Heartbeat Away," *Saturday Night* (February 1998), p. 36+.

Chapter Three

1. J.H.L. Playfair, *Immunology at a Glance*, 6th ed. (Oxford: Blackwell Science, 1996), p. 16.

2. A., V., and R. Silverstein, *The Circulatory System*, p. 49.

3. Ibid., p. 45.

4. Most sources agree on this estimate, but the Franklin Institute places the length in a child at 60,000 miles and in an adult at 100,000 miles.

5. A., V., and R. Silverstein, *The Circulatory System*, p. 37.

6. Avraham, *The Circulatory System*, p. 43.

7. Ibid., p. 49.

8. Nilsson, *The Body Victorious*, p. 50.

9. Dixie Farley, "The One-Two-Threes of a Complete Blood Count, Part 2," *FDA Consumer* (September 1989), pp. 28–32.

10. M.J. Wells and J. Wells, "Fluid Uptake and the Maintenance of Blood Volume in *Octopus*," *The Journal of Experimental Biology* (1993).

Chapter Four

1. D. M. Lloyd-Jones, M. G. Larson, A. Beiser, and D. Levy, "Lifetime Risk of Developing Coronary Heart Disease," *The Lancet* (January 9, 1999).

2. Y. Friedlander, D. S. Siscovick, S. Weinmann, M. A. Austin, B. M. Psaty, R. N. Lemaitre, P. Arbogast, T. E. Raghunathan, and L. A. Cobb, "Family History as a Risk Factor for Primary Cardiac Arrest," *Circulation* (January 20, 1998).

3. American Heart Association, *1999 Statistical Update*, p. 26.

4. American Heart Association, *Your Heart: An Owner's Manual* (Englewood Cliffs, NJ: Prentice Hall, 1995), p. 292.

5. B. Schumacher, P. Pecher, B.U. von Specht, and T. Stegmann, "Induction of Neoangiogenesis in Ischemic Myocardium by Human Growth Factors," *Circulation* (February 24, 1998).

6. E. Gurfinkel, G. Bozovich, A. Daroca, E. Beck, and B. Mautner, "Randomized Trial of Roxithromycin in Non-Q-Wave Coronary Syndromes: ROXIS Pilot Study," *The Lancet* (August 1997).

7. "Chest-Pain Units: A New Place for Coronary Care," *Harvard Heart Letter* (May 1999).

8. Dr. Jack Davis, Personal communication.

9. American Heart Association, *Your Heart: An Owner's Manual*, p. 12.

10. G. E. Cooke, P. F. Bray, J. D. Hamlington, D. M. Pham, P. J. Goldschmidt-Clermont, "P1A2 Polymorphism and Efficacy of Aspirin," *The Lancet* (April 25, 1998).

11. C. H. Hennekens, M. L. Dyken, and V. Fuster, "Aspirin as a Therapeutic Agent in Cardiovascular Disease: A Statement for Healthcare Professionals from the American Heart Association," *Circulation* (October 21, 1997).

12. A., V., and R. Silverstein, *The Circulatory System*, p. 75

13. Tom Reynolds, "Why Tumors Travel to Certain Sites Still Puzzles Researchers," *Journal of the National Cancer Institute* (April 1, 1998).

14. Ibid.

15. Evelyn Zamula, "Getting a Leg Up on Varicose Veins," *FDA Consumer* (February 1, 1990), pp. 24–28.

16. "Hypertension: New Guidelines, More Aggressive Treatment," *Mayo Health Oasis*, July 11, 1998.

17. N. S. Taylor-Tolbert, D. R. Dengel, M. D. Brown, S. D. McCole, R. E. Pratley, R. E. Farrell, and J. M. Hagberg, "Ambulatory Blood Pressure After Acute Exercise in Older Men with Essential Hypertension," *American Journal of Hypertension*, January 2000.

18. Y. Gidron, K. Davidson, and I. Bata, "The Short-Term Effects of a Hostility-Reduction Intervention on Male Coronary Heart Disease Patients," *Health Psychology*, July 1999.

19. "Heart Attack: The First Hour Can Be a Killer," *Mayo Health Clinic Letter*, May 1994.

20. Mark Buchanan, "The Heart That Just Won't Die," *New Scientist* (March 20, 1999).

Chapter Five

1. S. Wilcox and M. Stefanick, "Knowledge and Perceived Risk of Major Disease in Middle-Aged and Older Women," *Health Psychology* (July 1999).

2. F. Boulay, F. Berthier, O. Sisteron, Y. Gendreike, and P. Gibelin, "Seasonal Variation in Chronic Heart Failure Hospitalizations in France," *Circulation* (July 20, 1999).

3. P. M. Ridker, J. E. Buring, J. Shih, M. Matias, and C. H. Hennekens, "Prospective Study of C-Reactive Protein and the Risk of Future Cardiovascular Events among Apparently Healthy Women," *Circulation* (August 25, 1998).

4. S. Gottlieb, "Study Confirms Passive Smoking Increases Coronary Heart Disease," *British Medical Journal* (April 3, 1999).

5. M. Valkonen and T. Kuusi, "Passive Smoking Induces Atherogenic Changes in Low-Density Lipoprotein," *Circulation* (May 26, 1998).

6. "Cholesterol: Knowledge Behind Your Numbers," *Mayo Clinic Health Letter* (June 1993: updated by *Health Oasis*, September 24, 1998).

7. R. K. McCombs, D. E. Marcadis, J. Ellis, and R. B. Weinberg, "Attenuated Hypercholesterolemic Response to a High-Cholesterol Diet in Subjects Heterozygous for the Apolipoprotein A-IV-2 Allele," *The New England Journal of Medicine* (September 15, 1994).

8. American Heart Association, "Top 10 Research Advances of 1998"

9. R. J. Deckelbaum, E.A. Fisher, M. Winston, S. Kumanyika, R.M. Lauer, F.X. Pi-Sunyer, S. St. Joer, E.J. Schaefer, and I.B. Weinstein, "Unified Dietary Guidelines: Summary of a Consensus Conference on Preventive Nutrition: Pediatrics to Geriatrics," American Heart Association Reprint No. 71-0168.

10. L.F. Larsen, E.-M. Bladbjerg, J. Jespersen, and P. Marckmann, "Effects of Dietary Fat Quality and Quantity on Postprandial Activation of Blood Coagulation Factor VII," *Arteriosclerosis, Thrombosis, and Vascular Biology* (November 1997).

11. "Fat: Can You Go Too Low?" in "Medical News," *Family Circle* (September 15, 1998), p. 59.

12. "Obesity Now Recognized as a Major Risk Factor for Heart Disease and Stroke," *Mayo Health Oasis* (June 4, 1998). For the full story, see Robert H. Eckel and Ronald M. Kraus, "American Heart Association Call to Action: Obesity as a Major Risk Factor for Coronary Heart Disease," *Circulation* (June 2, 1998).

13. T. Dwyer, H. Iwane, K. Dean, Y. Odagiri, T. Shimomitsu, L. Blizzard, S. Srinivasan, T. Nicklas, W. Wattigney, M. Riley, and G. Berenson, "Differences in HDL Cholesterol Concentrations in Japanese, American, and Australian Children," *Circulation* (November 4, 1997).

14. N.F. Chu, E. B. Rimm, D. J. Wang, H.S. Liou, and S.M. Shieh, "Clustering of Cardiovascular Disease Risk Factors among Obese Schoolchildren: The Taipei Children Heart Study," *The American Journal of Clinical Nutrition* (June 1998), pp. 1141–1146.

15. "Vitamin and Nutritional Supplements: Sorting Out Fact from Fiction Amid a Storm of Controversy," *Medical Essay*, supplement to *Mayo Clinic Health Letter* (June 1997).

16. K. Robinson, K. Arheart, H. Refsum, L. Brattström, G. Boers, P. Ueland, P. Rubba, R. Palma-Reis, R. Meleady, L. Daly, J. Witteman, and I. Graham, "Low Circulating Folate and Vitamin B_6 Concentrations : Risk Factors for Stroke, Peripheral Vascular Disease, and Coronary Artery Disease," *Circulation* (February 10, 1998), pp. 437–443.

17. R. J. Shephard and G. J. Balady, "Exercise as Cardiovascular Therapy," *Circulation* (February 23, 1999).

18. I. M. Lee and R. S. Paffenbarger, "Physical Activity and Stroke Incidence: The Harvard Alumni Health Study," *Stroke* (October 1998).

19. A. A. Hakim, J. D. Curb, H. Petrovich, B. L. Rodriguez, K. Yano, G. W. Ross, L. R. White, and R. D. Abbott, "Effects of Walking on Coronary Heart Disease in Elderly Men: The Honolulu Heart Program," *Circulation* (July 6, 1999).

20. S. Kiechl, J. Willeit, G. Rungger, G. Egger, F. Oberhollenzer, and E. Bonora, "Alcohol Consumption and Atherosclerosis: What Is the Relation? : Prospective Results From the Bruneck Study," *Stroke* (May 1998).

21. C. M. Albert, J. E. Manson, N. R. Cook, U. A. Ajani, J. M. Gaziano, and C. H. Hennekens, "Moderate Alcohol Consumption and the Risk of Sudden Cardiac Death Among U.S. Male Physicians," *Circulation* (August 31, 1999).

22. C. L. Hart, G. D. Smith, D. J. Hole, and V. M. Hawthorne, "Alcohol Consumption and Mortality from All Causes, Coronary Heart Disease, and Stroke: Results from a Prospective Cohort Study of Scottish Men with 21 Years of Follow Up," *British Medical Journal* (June 26, 1999), pp.1725–1729.

23. Kiechl et al., *Stroke*, (May 1998).

24. "The Pill Revisited: Benefits Beyond Birth Control," *Mayo Clinic's Women's Health Source* (August 1998).

25. Adapted from the U.S. Department of Health and Human Services, Public Health Service, National Institutes of Health Publication Nos. 93-2724, 95-3794, and 95-3795.

26. American Heart Association, *1999 Heart and Stroke Statistical Update*, p. 3.

GLOSSARY

Adrenaline: Also called epinephrine, a hormone produced by the adrenal gland that stimulates the pacemaker to increase heart rate.

Aerobic exercise: Exercise strenuous enough to increase breathing rate and heart rate, thereby building strength in heart and lungs.

Albumin: A protein in blood plasma that prevents excessive bleeding.

Alveolus: (Plural is alveoli.) Air sacs in the lungs where carbon dioxide and oxygen are exchanged between blood and inhaled air.

Amino acids: The building-block molecules from which proteins are made.

Anemia: An insufficiency of the oxygen-carrying molecule hemoglobin or in the number of red blood cells or a depleted total volume of blood.

Aneurysm: A weak spot in an artery that may balloon or burst.

Angina: Chest pain resulting from an inadequate supply of blood to the heart muscle.

Angiogram: A diagnostic test that uses X rays to detect a dye moving through blood vessels and heart chambers, to reveal any defects and abnormalities in structure and flow.

Angioplasty: Removing plaque to open a blocked artery using a balloon, laser, or other method.

Antibody: A protein made by the immune system that combats invading disease-causing organisms.

Anticoagulant: A substance that prevents blood from clotting or dissolves clots.

Antigen: A protein in blood. (In other contexts, the term is often used to describe proteins that induce allergic reactions.)

Antioxidant: Any of a number of substances including plant hormones and certain vitamins that prevent free radicals (charged molecules) from combining with oxygen and therefore inflicting damage on artery walls.

Aorta: The largest artery in the body, it runs out of the left ventricle and supplies blood to the torso, arms, and legs.

Aortic valve: The three-flapped heart valve that lies between the left ventricle and the aorta.

Arteriography: An imaging technique in which dyes in the bloodstream show up on X rays to reveal damage in arteries.

Arteriosclerosis: The hardening, thickening, and loss of elasticity in artery walls that comes with age.

Arterioles: The smallest arteries.

Artery: Blood vessels that carry blood away from the heart.

Atherosclerosis: A chronic condition in which damaged artery walls become blocked with plaque, which impairs the flow of blood.

Atrioventricular (A-V) node: A bundle of nerve and muscle tissue located between the atria and the ventricles in the heart that receives electrical impulses from the sinoatrial (S-A) node and regulates the rate of the heartbeat.

Atrium: Either of the heart's two upper chambers.

Bilirubin: A by-product of the breakdown of hemoglobin that causes jaundice.

Biofeedback: A technique of relaxation and learning by which people can learn to control normally involuntary actions such as heart rate or blood pressure.

Blood pressure: The force exerted by blood in the arteries.

Bone marrow: The spongy tissue inside the bones responsible for the formation of blood cells.

Bypass surgery: An operation that repairs or circumvents damaged coronary arteries to improve the blood supply to the heart muscle.

Calorie: The unit that measures the energy in food. (Also called a kilocalorie.)

Carbohydrate: A category of chemicals that includes compounds made of carbon, hydrogen, and oxygen. A major category of food.

Cardiovascular exercise: Physical activity intense enough to strengthen the circulatory system.

Capillaries: The thin-walled, smallest blood vessels that lie between an arteriole and a venule and allow diffusion of molecules back and forth between blood and tissues.

Cardiopulmonary Resuscitation (CPR): Chest compression and mouth-to-mouth air exchange used as first aid for any cessation of heartbeat or breathing.

Catheterization: A method of examining the heart by passing a thin tube (catheter) into the heart through a vein or artery.

Cholesterol: A fatlike substance produced in the liver and plentiful in fatty foods from animal sources (such as meat, whole milk, and egg yolks).

Circulatory system: The heart, blood, and blood vessels.

Clot: A mass of fibers, cells, and tissue formed by clotting factors in the blood. Clots stop the flow of blood from injuries, but may also form inside an artery, where they can cause heart attack or stroke.

Complement: Also called complement series. A group of some fifteen enzymes in blood that react as part of the body's immune response to invading microorganisms or foreign proteins.

Coronary arteries: The blood vessels that supply blood to the heart muscle.

Defibrillator: An electronic device used to slow rapid heart rates to normal.

Diabetes: A disease caused by the production of too little insulin in the pancreas. Lacking insulin, the body cannot properly extract energy from sugar in the blood.

Diastole: The relaxation phase of the heartbeat that yields the second (smaller) number of blood pressure measurement.

Echocardiography: An examination of the heart using ultrasound waves to produce a picture of the heart's structure, size, and contractions.

Electrocardiogram (ECG or EKG): A graph of the heart's electrical impulses.

Embolus: A blood clot that moves through the bloodstream and may lodge in a vital organ such as the heart (causing a heart attack) or the brain (causing a stroke).

Embolism: An obstruction of a blood vessel caused by a clot or other mass.

Enzyme: A protein that speeds up biochemical reactions in cells.

Epinephrine: See adrenaline.

Erythrocytes: See red blood cells.

Estrogen: A female hormone.

Fat: A general term for chemicals that are glycerides of fatty acids. A category of energy-rich foods that includes butter, margarine, and vegetable oils.

Fibrillation: Uncoordinated contractions of the heart.

Fibrin: Fibrous, clot-forming material in the blood.

Fibrinogen: A protein in blood that is essential to clotting.

Free radical: A charged molecule that can damage body cells when combined with oxygen.

Glucose: The simple sugar the body uses for energy.

Glycogen: A carbohydrate produced by the liver that stores energy in the body.

Heart attack: An interruption or cessation of heart action, usually due to a blockage of the blood supply to the heart muscle, resulting in subsequent death of part of the muscle tissue.

Heart disease: A condition involving the blockage of coronary arteries with plaque.

Hematocrit: A measure of relative proportion of solids in blood.

Hemocyanin: An copper-containing, oxygen-binding molecule that occurs in the blood of some animals.

Hemoglobin: The iron-containing pigment in the red blood cells and some other animals that carries oxygen and makes blood red.

Hemophilia: An inherited disorder of blood clotting.

High-Density Lipoprotein (HDL): The "good" cholesterol. A molecule that removes cholesterol from the blood by carrying it to the liver for disposal.

Hypertension: High blood pressure.

Immune system: The leukocytes, enzymes, antibodies and other mechanisms that defend the body against disease.

Inflammation: The swelling, redness, pain, heat, and stiffness of an infection or injury resulting from actions of the immune system.

Ion: Charged atom or small molecule.

Ischemia: Reduced circulation in a part of the body. A drop in blood flow to an organ, usually due to a blockage of an artery.

Jaundice: Yellowing of the skin.

Leukemia: A category of blood diseases involving excessive numbers of white blood cells.

Leukocytes: See white blood cells.

Low-Density Lipoprotein (LDL): The "bad" cholesterol. The carrier of cholesterol that contributes to the formation of plaque in artery walls.

Lymph: The clear fluid that bathes body cells and circulates outside of arteries and veins.

Lymphocyte: A type of white blood cell involved in the immune response.

• *Lymphoma*: A kind of cancer in which abnormal lymphocytes increase in number. They crowd out healthy cells and grow tumors in lymph nodes. (Hodgkin's disease is one kind of lymphoma.)

Metabolism: The rate at which energy is released from food inside body cells.

Monounsaturated fat: Found in canola, olive, and peanut oils.

Myeloma: A type of cancer in which plasma cells multiply out of control, destroying bone marrow and interfering with the manufacture of blood cells and antibodies.

Pacemaker: See sinoatrial (S-A) node. Electric pacemakers may be implanted surgically when the heart's natural pacemaker fails.

Perfusionist: A medical worker who operates a heart/lung machine.

Phlebitis: Blockage and inflammation in a vein.

Plaque: Deposits of fat, cholesterol, and other substances in an artery wall.

Plasma: The liquid portion of blood made of water and dissolves salts, proteins, and lipids.

Plasma cell: A type of white blood cell involved in the immune response.

Platelets: Cells in the blood essential to clotting.

Polyunsaturated fats: Fats that are liquid at room temperature and found primarily in vegetable oils such as safflower, sunflower, and soybean.

Protein: Chemicals composed of amino acids. A major food group, which includes meats, eggs, peanut butter, and soybeans.

Pulmonary: Pertaining to the lungs.

Red blood cells: Blood cells that contain hemoglobin and carry oxygen.

Rh factor: A protein present in some people's blood that can produce a rejection response if transfused into someone normally lacking the factor.

Risk factor: Any influences such as heredity or lifestyle habits that increase the chances of an event occurring (such as a heart attack).

Saturated fats: Fats that are solid at room temperature, including animal fats, butter, and vegetable fats that have been treated to make them hard (as in some margarines).

Serum: The liquid portion of blood minus clotting factors such as fibrinogen.

Shock: A rapid drop in blood pressure resulting from blood loss.

Sickle-cell disease: An inherited disorder involving misshapen blood cells with a reduced capacity to carry oxygen.

Sinoatrial (S-A) node: A bundle of nerve and muscle tissue in the right atrium that sends out electrical impulses that regulate the heart's contraction. See also atrioventricular (A-V) node.

Stem cells: The "mother cells" from which all types of blood cells are formed.

Stress: Mental or physical tension brought on by emotional factors or physical overexertion.

Stroke: Loss of some part of brain function resulting from the blockage of blood supply to brain tissue.

Stroke volume: The amount of blood the heart pumps with each beat.

Systole: The contraction phase of the heartbeat that yields the first (larger) number of blood pressure measurement.

Sympathetic nerve: A nerve that carries signals from the brain that speed heart rate.

Thrombin: A chemical released by platelets that converts fibrinogen into fibrin to form blood clots.

Thrombosis: The formation of blood clots inside coronary arteries.

Thrombus: A blood clot or other blockage attached to the wall of a blood vessel.

Thyroxine: A hormone made by the thyroid gland that regulates the use of food in body cells (metabolism)

Triglyceride: A fat in food or made by the body from other foods.

Vagus nerve: A nerve that carries signals from the brain which slow the heart rate.

Vein: A blood vessel that returns blood to the heart.

Venules: The smallest veins.

Ventricle: One of the two lower chambers of the heart.

Ventricular fibrillation: A rapid and nonproductive contraction of the lower heart chamber.

White blood cells: Cells in the blood of several different types that fight disease and provide immunity.

FOR FURTHER INFORMATION

BOOKS

American Heart Association. *Your Heart: An Owner's Manual*. Englewood Cliffs, NJ: Prentice Hall, 1995.

Ballard, Carol. *The Human Body: The Heart and Circulatory System*. Austin, TX: Raintree Steck-Vaughn, 1997.

Bryan, Jenny. *Body Talk: The Pulse of Life: The Circulatory System*. New York: Dillon Press, 1992.

Brynie, Faith Hickman. *101 Questions About Your Immune System That You Felt Defenseless to Answer…Until Now*. Brookfield, CT: Twenty-First Century Books, 1999.

DeBakey, Michael E., M.D. and Antonio M. Gotto Jr., M.D. *The New Living Heart*. Holbrook, MA: Adams Media Corporation, 1997.

Gersh, Bernard J., ed. *Mayo Clinic Heart Book*, Second Edition. New York: William Morrow, 2000.

Kowalski, Robert E. *8 Steps to a Healthy Heart: The Complete Guide to Heart Disease Prevention and Recovery From Heart Attack and Bypass Surgery*. New York: Warner Books, 1992.

National Geographic Society. *The Incredible Machine*. Washington, DC: National Geographic Society, 1986.

Silverstein, Alvin; Virginia Silverstein, and Robert Silverstein. *The Circulatory System*. Brookfield, CT: Twenty-First Century Books, 1994.

ARTICLES

Brink, Susan. "Unlocking the Heart's Secrets." *U.S. News and World Report* (September 9, 1998), p. 58.

Browder, Sue Ellen. "A Woman's Heart." *Woman's Day* (February 17, 1998), p. 42.

Brownlee, Shannon. "Can't Do Without Love." *U.S. News and World Report* (February 17, 1997), p. 58.

Cool, Lisa Collier. "Brain Attack!" *Good Housekeeping* (December 1999), p.64.

Dyson, Marianne J. "Have a Heart." *Odyssey* (September 1999), p. 27.

Fischman, Josh. "Why We Fall in Love." *U.S. News & World Report* (February 7, 2000), p. 42.

Murphy, Todd. "Women and Heart Disease." *Better Homes and Gardens* (September 1998), p. 106.

Regalado, Antonio. "CPR for the Artificial Heart." *Technology Review*, May/June 1999.

"The Science of Love." *Life* (February 1999), p. 38.

On the Internet:

Ask the experts at Columbia University your question about health at http://www.goaskalice.columbia.edu

Take the Mayo Clinic's "Interactive Heart Tour" at http://www.mayohealth.org/mayo/9902/htm/heart/heart.htm. Read one man's story of his heart attack at "Life after Sudden Death," http://www.mayohealth.org/mayo/9811/htm/sudden_wwb.htm.

Explore the heart with the Franklin Institute Science Museum at http://sln2.fi.edu/biosci/heart.html.

The University of Wisconsin "Why Files" invite you to hear the heart's beat at http://news3.news.wisc.edu/028heart/how_works1.html.

AGENCIES AND ORGANIZATIONS

American College of Sports Medicine
P.O. Box 1440
Indianapolis, IN 46206-1440
Publishes *Health and Fitness Journal* bimonthly.
http://www.acsm.org

American Diabetes Association
1701 North Beauregard Street
Alexandria, VA 22311
Publishes the health and wellness magazine *Diabetes Forecast* monthly.
http://www.diabetes.org/ada/info.asp

American Heart Association National Center
7272 Greenville Avenue
Dallas, TX 75231-4596
Publishes low-fat cookbooks, lifestyle guides, and Spanish-language brochures.
http://www.americanheart.org

American Lung Association
1740 Broadway
New York, NY 10019-4374
Publishes *Breathe Easy, The Weekly Breather,* and several other online newsletters.
http://www.lungusa.org

American Red Cross
Attn: Public Inquiry Office
11th Floor
1621 N. Kent Street
Arlington, VA 22209
Ask about their blood, plasma, and stem-cell programs, as well as disaster relief.
http://www.redcross.org

America's Blood Centers
725 15th Street NW, Suite 700
Washington, DC 20005
Serves 46 states with more than 450 blood donation sites.
www.americasblood.org

Federation of American Societies for Experimental Biology
Office of Public Affairs
9650 Rockville Pike
Bethesda, MD 20814-3998
Request a reprint of "Cardiovascular Disease and the Endothelium," by Jeffrey Porro, an article from the federation's "Breakthroughs in Bioscience" series.
http://www.faseb.org

International Society for Heart and Lung Transplantation
14673 Midway Road, Suite 200
Addison, TX 75001
Publishes the *Journal of Heart and Lung Transplantation*
http://www.ishlt.org

International Food Information Council
1100 Connecticut Avenue NW, Suite 430
Washington, DC 20036
Find out the latest in scientific research on food and nutrition.
http://ificinfo.health.org

Leukemia Society of America
600 Third Avenue
New York, NY 10016
Call the society's Information Resource Center at 1-800-955-4LSA.
http://www.leukemia.org

National Cholesterol Education Program
Information Center
4733 Bethesda Avenue
Bethesda, MD 20814-4820
Provides heart-smart nutrition information to health-care professionals and the public.
http://www.nhlbi.nih.gov/about/ncep/index.htm

National Health Information Center
Office of Disease Prevention and Health Promotion
U.S. Public Health Service
Department of Health and Human Services
Humphrey Building, Room 738 G
200 Independence Avenue SW
Washington, DC 20201
Publishes goals for the health of the nation and nutrition guidelines.
http://odphp.osophs.dhhs.gov

National Heart, Lung, and Blood Institute
NHLBI Information Center
P.O. Box 30105
Bethesda, MD 20824-0105
Call the Heart Health Information line at 1-800-575-WELL.
http://www.nhlbi.nih.gov/health/infoctr/index.htm

National Hemophilia Foundation
116 West 32nd Street, 11th Floor
New York, NY 10001
Publishes a *Community Alert* newsletter.
www.hemophilia.org

President's Council on Physical Fitness and Sports
701 Pennsylvania Avenue NW
Suite 250
Washington, DC 20004
Publishes a quarterly newsletter and guides on exercise.
http://www.surgeongeneral.gov/ophs/pcpfs.htm

Sickle-Cell Disease Association of America
National Headquarters
200 Corporate Pointe, Suite 495
Culver City, CA 90230-8727
Publications for patients, physicians, students, and families.
www.sicklecelldisease.org

INDEX

Page numbers in *italics* refer to illustrations.